QUESTING

QUESTING:

A KINGDOM RECALIBRATION

WAYNE BERRY

WordCrafts

Questing: A Kingdom Recalibration
Copyright © 2022
Wayne Berry

ISBN: 978-1-957344-31-7

Cover concept and design by Jonathan Grisham for Grisham Designs

Published by WordCrafts Press
Cody, Wyoming 82414
www.wordcrafts.net

"And whatever you do, in word or deed, do everything in the name of the Lord Jesus, giving thanks to God the Father through him."

~Col. 3:17

To the Almighty God, Sovereign Creator of the universe (Eph. 4:6); Jesus Christ, my Lord, and Savior who sits at the right hand of the Father, ever interceding for all the saints (Rom. 8:34); and to honor the presence, power, and purpose of the Holy Ghost.

But ye shall receive power [after] that the Holy Ghost is come upon you: and ye shall [be] witnesses unto me both in Jerusalem, and in all Judaea, and in Samaria, and unto the uttermost part of the earth.

~Acts 1:8 (KJV) emphasis added

Presence precedes Power
Power produces Witness
Witness proclaims Testimony
Testimony prompts Revival

And to my family, as a road map to help guide them along the highway to Zion. (Ps. 84:5-7)

This is a work in progress…from where I am to where I'm going.

QUESTING: A KINGDOM RECALIBRATION

"These all died in faith, not having received the promises, but having seen them afar off, and were persuaded of them, and embraced them, and confessed that they were strangers and pilgrims on the earth."

~Heb. 11:13 (KJV)

PUBLISHED ON PURPOSE:

When the Holy Ghost prompts you in a given direction, you have three basic choices:
- Disregard/Disobey
- Pause/Postpone
- Follow/Submit

During my life I have done all three. This manuscript is directly linked to my yielding to the choice to follow Him. It has to do with the process of clarification and consideration related to the why's, what's, and how's that transpire when attempting to pursue what Jesus said was to be the #1 priority in the lives of those who purpose to follow after Him:

"Seek first the kingdom of God and His righteousness…"

~Mt. 6:33

Contents

Introduction

This is a personal theological narrative based on four specific aspects of the kingdom of God:
- What it is
- How to get in
- The price of participation
- The practice of the process (Citizenship / Reconciliation / Ambassadorship)

Each section will focus in on one of the themes of each of these particular four points. I will try my best to stay on topic, but I make no promises in that regard.

> *Sometimes the best map will not guide you*
> *You can't see what's round the bend*
> *Sometimes the road leads through dark places*
> *Sometimes the darkness is your friend*
>
> (B. Cockburn)

Here are some *GPS coordinates for the sojourn ahead.
*Gospel Positioning System

"How precious is your steadfast love, O God! The children of mankind take refuge in the shadow of your wings. They feast on the abundance of your house, and you give them drink from

the river of your delights. For with you is the fountain of life; in your light do we see light."

~Ps. 36:7-9

"Blessed are those whose strength is in you, in whose heart are the highways to Zion."

~Ps. 84:5

"Your word is a lamp to my feet and a light to my path."
~Ps. 119:105

"Where shall I go from your Spirit? Or where shall I flee from your presence? If I ascend to heaven, you are there! If I make my bed in Sheol, you are there! If I take the wings of the morning and dwell in the uttermost parts of the sea, even there your hand shall lead me, and your right hand shall hold me. If I say,' Surely the darkness shall cover me, and the light about me be night,' even the darkness is not dark to you; the night is bright as the day, for darkness is as light with you."

~Ps. 139:7-12

"But the path of the righteous is like the light of dawn, which shines brighter and brighter until full day."

~Pro. 4:18

"I will give you the treasures of darkness and the hoards in secret places, that you may know that it is I, the Lord, the God of Israel, who called you by your name."

~Isa. 45:3

"Every good gift and every perfect gift is from above, coming down from the Father of lights, with whom there is no variation or shadow due to change."

~Ja. 1:17

Preface

In March of 2018, in a service in South Africa, the Lord planted a creative seed in my word-womb.

He is the creative force of creativity itself. Creativity is the first known attribute that He presented of Himself. *In the beginning God created…"* (Gen. 1:1), and *"Every good gift and every perfect gift is from above, and cometh down from the Father of lights, with whom is no variableness, neither shadow of turning"* (Ja. 1:17). God is the source of the seed. Jesus is the Nurturer, through His mercy, grace, and steadfast intercession on behalf of those who follow Him (Heb. 7:25). And, the Holy Spirit has served as a sort of Midwife for the last three and a half years.

Over the last several weeks, there has been a lot of internal movement taking place. And then, this morning, the pace of delivery quickened, and the new arrival began to travel down the birth canal—crowning just before dawn. Here are the details of conception: The seed mentioned above came in the form of one singular word—*recalibration*. When inception took place, the Spirit provided no more information, just that one word. I've had previous experiences with that exact process before. On more than one occasion, the Lord has given me a word to ponder. Then, over time, through prayerful interaction, additional data began to be imparted and deposited inside of me. I understood the process, but, I didn't know how the word

recalibration was meant to be applied. So, I began to pray for clarity from the Holy Ghost regarding its meaning and appropriation.

For weeks (months really), I turned that one word over, up, and around in my mind, trying to sort out what the Lord was saying. Those ponderings then were fashioned into a simple and ongoing prayer—*Lord, what does that mean?*

After about three months or thereabouts, I found myself considering where the term *recalibration* was most currently used. I realized that I related it mostly to what takes place when a GPS system is being reset. When the device needs current coordinates to provide clear directions for a specific destination, a voice says that it is "recalibrating." That seemed like a possible application for consideration. So, I added that to my prayer by asking the Lord if that had anything to do with what He had spoken to me. At that point, the interchanges got very interesting.

The Holy Spirit brought Mt. 6:33 to mind, prompting me to factor in what it said: *"Seek first the kingdom of God and his righteousness…"*

When that occurred, I asked the Lord how that verse related to me in terms of recalibration. Then, the entire process which had been at work for some five months or so came into full focus. The Holy Ghost said, "You need to recalibrate your life in terms of Mt. 6:33."

At that point the real struggle began: I started to think that I had been missing the calling of the Lord, perhaps for decades, since the main focus of my life and ministry had been the creative aspects of music (singing, playing, composing, arranging, team leadership, teaching, and writing). If people who knew me were asked what my ministry was, they would have said something related directly to those categories of service. So, prepared to confess and repent for what may have been my lack of obedience, I asked the Lord if I had missed His will. The response was quick in coming, and comforting to my soul. The Spirit said, "I didn't say you needed to repent. I said you needed to recalibrate."

From here, I could go on for a long time, with lots of details as to how all that has been outworking for the last 3 ½ years. But, I think a short response will serve to establish how this manuscript has come to be. I took the Spirit's direction to heart, and placed Mt. 6:33 at the very top of my "to do" list. However, how I apply the things of the Kingdom has been altered/altared by the events I've just explained.

Since March of 2017, I've transitioned from retirement, to rebootment, to recalibration (ongoing). My first priority now, and for the rest of my life, is that of seeking the kingdom of God and His righteousness. This book is part of that process.

KINGDOM LIFE

Spirit come and take control
Touch me deep down in my soul
Fill me till I overflow, with kingdom life

Speak to me and I'll obey
Every word I hear You say
Lead me in Your righteous way
To kingdom life

I long to be like You
In everything I say and do
But I can't live that life
Without your presence deep inside

Father, Son, and Holy Ghost
Grant me what I'm needing most
The spirit of the Pentecost for kingdom life
~W. Berry / See & Say Songs, BMI

DISCLAIMER: Throughout this manuscript I will be including quotes from other people and sources. When I do, I am not directly affirming the individuals or their work as such. Rather, I'll share a specific quoted thought because it states something that I personally AMEN, having confirmed or validated what I could have said. They just said it first, or better. *Capisce?*

Unless noted otherwise, all Scriptural quotes are from the English Standard Version. Permission has been secured in writing from the various publishers for all footnoted quotes.

Section One
THE QUEST

THE KINGDOM IS THE CONTEXT

Every word in Scripture, every principle, precept, process, and practice, is linked (one way or another) to a Kingdom context. That is to say they are rooted in, and growing from the foundation of God's kingdom. I am aware that such a statement is filled with all kinds of implications, along with the potential for gross misunderstandings. So, before I go any further with this manuscript, I need to make an attempt to clarify why I've made such comments as these.

The Bible is filled with words. The words are seeds (Lu. 8:11-18). I'll expound on that after I address the topic of context in more detail.

The words contained in Scripture form phrase s, sentences, and paragraphs. They are presented in verses. There are 31,102 verses in the Bible. The verses are gathered together in chapters. There are 1,189 chapters in the Bible. Each chapter is presented in a book. There are sixty-six books in the Bible. Each chapter provides a context for the content it contains. Each chapter is collected into

the context of a book. Each book contains the content of each chapter. All of the word content is located in the context of a chapter. All the content of each chapter is contained in the context of a book. And, all the content contained in all sixty-six books is gathered into the context of the Biblical canon—the Holy Bible.

In essence, any and all the word content in Scripture provides a manual (textbook) that addresses each and every dynamic aspect of the kingdom of God. The Bible is the guidebook for Kingdom living.

I consider Myles Munroe's book, *Understanding Your Place In God's Kingdom* to be one of the most important contemporary works in print regarding the pursuit of insight and application concerning the kingdom of God. In relationship to establishing a Kingdom context, he states:

"In particular terms, a kingdom may be defined as 'the sovereign rule of a king over territory (domain), impacting it with his will, purpose, and intent…the kingdom of God means God's will executed, Gods' jurisdiction, heaven's influence, God's administration, and God's impact and influence…it is the governing influence of a king over his territory, producing a culture, values, morals, and lifestyle that reflect the king's desires and nature for his citizens.'"

Munroe continues, "…God established only two priorities for mankind: *the Kingdom of God and the righteousness of God.* Kingdom refers to the governing influence of Heaven on earth and righteousness refers to right alignment and positioning with that government authority. Our highest priorities and greatest desires should be to enter the Kingdom of God and thirst for a right relationship with God's heavenly government."

In his book, *Cosmic Initiative,* Jack Taylor emphasizes the centrality of God's kingdom by inviting his readers to "seek the kingdom, to understand it, and to live in its reality." Stating, "travelers can't have too much information when they embark on a significant journey." He sees questing for and dwelling in God's kingdom as "the most momentous journey of life."

"The basic meaning of the word *kingdom* in the Bible is God's reign, not realm, or people. The kingdom creates a realm, but, it is not synonymous with its realm or its people." (John Piper)

The Lord has established his throne in the heavens, and his kingdom rules over all. (Ps. 103:19)

In regards to prioritizing the Kingdom as number one—based on Mt. 6:33, E. Stanley Jones makes the following observations:

"The central and acute sickness of this age is that people do not belong—do not belong to anything significant..."

Considering that his comments were made over half a century ago, think how much more that condition applies to the world we live in today.

He goes on to say, "...the Church has lost the kingdom of God... and it is largely to blame because instead of offering the kingdom of God it has offered various conflicts—fundamentalist-modernist; the social gospel-the individual gospel; racial integration; the secular church; long hair-short hair; beards and non-beards; the church building orgy; then vestments and candles and robes; conversion; abolition of poverty and the ghettos—every issue except the kingdom of God...if the kingdom of God is missing in the magnificent and in the minute, then the key to meaning, goal, life-redemption, and life-fulfillment is missing. Life turns meaningless and sick, becomes a problem instead of a possibility. But, if you have the key of the kingdom, you find it a master-key, the key to life now and hereafter, life individual and collective... for the Church to be relevant the answer is simple: Discover the kingdom, surrender to the kingdom, make the kingdom your life and your life program; then in everything and everywhere you will be relevant. For the kingdom of God is relevance—ultimate and final relevance. And, when you have it, and it has you, then you are relevancy itself...the Church having lost its absolute—the kingdom of God—it is now in a welter of conflicting relativism, all bidding for the Church's attention and loyalty. So the Church leaves a blur instead of a mark. Where Paul could say, "This one

thing I do," the Church says, "These forty things I dabble in." The Church needs nothing so much as it needs a rediscovery of the absolute, the absolute of the kingdom, that would bring life back into unity, point it to new goals, individual and collective, discover new power, the power of the Spirit, to move on to those goals, and give it nerve to face a hesitating and confused world with—repent for the kingdom of God is at hand…we do not seek first, last, and always the kingdom of God as our way of life now,, and we do not offer it to the world as our answer to the world's ills now. What we have lost is **God's redemptive totalitarianism**, the kingdom of God. That is the central sickness of our age." (emphasis added)

Again, keep in mind that those comments are from 1972. As I survey the daze we're living in, I read them as prophetically-insightful declarations.

"The kingdom of God is God's reign in man's heart through Jesus Christ. In other words, God's kingdom is God's redemptive aeon in and through Jesus His Son." (George Dana Boardman)

Jack Taylor offers his narrative as to how realigning his theology in the context of God's kingdom transformed his spiritual understanding:

"I started to see the kingdom of God as the center of my faith and theology, but even more than that, I saw it as 'everything' that mattered and inclusive of everything I had ever known and everything I would ever learn about God and His sovereign rule. I now understand it as the wholeness of a kingdom perspective. What became the focus of my thinking cast its blessed shadow from center to circumference and brought new meaning to each individual part of the picture…it became the key to personal and cultural transformation."

"God's kingdom is nothing if not cosmic; it covers all that exists, everywhere—past, present, and future; visible and invisible." (Jack Taylor)

"The kingdom of God is the eternal rule of God over everything and everybody, everywhere, for all time and eternity. It is above time yet envelops time; it transcends time and endures time. A

million billion ages ago, God's kingdom existed; a million billion years from now, it will still exist. Being eternally permanent, it wins the right to be 'everything,' because everything else is either encompassed by it—or will ultimately cease to be." (Jack Taylor)

S.D. Gordon understands the timelessness of God's kingdom as existing in "the beginningless beginning." That phrase resonates with me—big time.

> *"Where shall I go from your Spirit? Or where shall I flee from your presence? If I ascend to heaven, you are there! If I make my bed in Sheol, you are there! If I take the wings of the morning and dwell in the uttermost parts of the sea, even there your hand shall lead me, and your right hand shall hold me. If I say, 'Surely the darkness shall cover me, and the light about me be night,' even the darkness is not dark to you; the night is bright as the day, for darkness is as light with you."*
>
> ~Ps. 139:7-12

Taylor sees the Kingdom as providing a context for five key aspects of life here on earth:
- A renewed sense of purpose for individual believers
- A revitalized role for the church in the world
- The healing of society's ills
- The active proclamation the gospel message with songs following
- A hopeful view of the future of humanity

He believes we are to "seek the Kingdom as a present lifestyle." So do I. That's why I've written this manuscript.

SEEDING THE KINGDOM

> *"Soon afterward he went on through cities and villages, proclaiming and bringing the good news of the kingdom of God..."*
>
> ~Lu. 8:1-15

The Parable of the Sower

...and when a great crowd was gathering and people from town after town came to him, he said in a parable, "A sower went out to sow his seed. And as he sowed, some fell along the path and was trampled underfoot, and the birds of the air devoured it. And some fell on the rock, and as it grew up, it withered away, because it had no moisture. And some fell among thorns, and the thorns grew up with it and choked it. And some fell into good soil and grew and yielded a hundredfold." As he said these things, he called out, "He who has ears to hear, let him hear."

The Purpose of the Parables

And when his disciples asked him what this parable meant, he said, "To you it has been given to know the secrets of the kingdom of God, but for others they are in parables, so that 'seeing they may not see, and hearing they may not understand. Now the parable is this: The seed is the word of God. The ones along the path are those who have heard; then the devil comes and takes away the word from their hearts, so that they may not believe and be saved. And the ones on the rock are those who, when they hear the word, receive it with joy. But these have no root; they believe for a while, and in time of testing fall away. And as for what fell among the thorns, they are those who hear, but as they go on their way they are choked by the cares and riches and pleasures of life, and their fruit does not mature. As for that in the good soil, they are those who, hearing the word, hold it fast in an honest and good heart, and bear fruit with patience."

~Lu. 8:1-15

The soil where seeds are planted doesn't provide the roots. The roots are contained inside of the seed. The environment (soil) where seeds are planted helps nurture the seed into maturity. Without

13

the proper environment, the seed will remain barren, dormant, and unable to produce (or reproduce) in kind. That is to say, the roots of a thing are not found in the ground where it's planted. Rather, its roots are contained in the seed that produces (or releases) it into life-bearing. The thing that's planted is not born from the environment where it is to grow. Its life is in the seed that contains it, not in the soil that helps sustain it. Such is the case with Kingdom seed. Consider this:

KINGDOM FEED , SEED (AN ANALOGY) PART 1

"Those who sow in tears shall reap with shouts of joy! He who goes out weeping, bearing the seed for sowing, shall come home with shouts of joy, bringing his sheaves with him."

~Ps. 126:5, 6

I have an open account at my local KINGDOM FEED , SEED store. I've been running a tab there for decades. I'm told that as long as I continue to pick up my supplies there my account will remain open and active. The owners are gracious that way.

I've purchased lots of different resources there, but the main one is *Word-seed. I go there regularly in order to make certain that I have plenty of seed for sowing. That's because I never know for certain when I'll find myself in a field that's ready for planting. So as not to be caught short, I've learned to keep my bag as full as possible—just in case it's needed.

I can't sow what I don't have. If I'm Word deficient, then my ability to sow Word-seed is diminished. And, limited sowing will produce limited croPs. And, limited crops will in turn produce a limited harvest. And, a limited harvest will impact my personal ability to reap with shouts of joy.

See how that works?

*"...*the seed is the word of God.*"*

~Lu. 8:11b

14

Kingdom Feed , Seed (An Analogy) Part 2

"Those who sow in tears shall reap with shouts of joy! He who goes out weeping, bearing the seed for sowing, shall come home with shouts of joy, bringing his sheaves with him."

~Ps. 126:5, 6

Sow what?

There are two basic kinds of seeds:

Temporal—Meant for sowing on earth. Such seeds produce a temporary yield that is useful for life on the planet. Its shelf-life extends from the cradle to the grave. Its sell-by date is based on the length of the lives of those who have the opportunity to partake of its harvest.

Eternal—Meant for use while on earth (in a temporal environment), but also for use off site in the realm of the everlasting. Its yield is forever constant.

While both types of seed are important, only one is worthwhile on earth, and also into eternity.

When sowing either seed, the fields they are scattered into depend on two key aspects:

How prepared the Sowers are as to when there is a field available.

How much seed the Sowers keep with them.

In many cases, those who sow don't have a direct input as to what fields they find themselves in. That being the case, it is the responsibility of those who carry seed to be ready for sowing whenever and wherever they find the circumstances right for distributing what they carry in their seed bag.

For example, I have the opportunity to sow into a few Social Media fields, not of my choosing. Nonetheless, I find myself standing in such fields most days. Another field is narrative publication—this book. In fact, you are passing through that field at this very moment.

Selah (pause , ponder)

Add this to that: Everything on earth is in process. EVERY-THING (the earth itself / all of creation—including nature, humankind, history, and the cosmos itself). Every single process is framed within the context of earth-time. Earth-time has a beginning, middle, and end—from sunrise to sunset—the "in the beginning" of the beginning (Gen. 1:1). So, every process starts at some point, and ends at some point.

We can try to will away (or opt out) of the process. But such attempts are unworkable. Those endeavors are all framed (contained) within the context of time. Perhaps some sort of clever invention or productive idea may be implemented in order to alter the process—perhaps even bring it to an end. However, that too takes time.

Are you seeing a pattern here?

Whatever the conditions or circumstances that are taking place may be, they can only transition from beginning to end through the process of time. So, how each of us relates to and processing time is critical to how we ourselves transition. Scripture has much to say regarding time. I'll include my two favorite Biblically-based statements about that, and continue on my way:

> *But I trust in you, O Lord; I say, "You are my God." My times are in your hand…*
>
> ~Ps. 31:4-15a

> *So teach us to number our days that we may get a heart of wisdom.*
>
> ~Ps. 90:12

SEEING THE KINGDOM

There are two basic ways to look at life: one is from here, and the other is from hereafter.

The view from here is temporal, based on earth time, and passing

away. Life seen from this viewpoint has a beginning, middle, and end. It is framed (bookended) by birth on one end, and death on the other. Looking at life from this perspective takes place through earthly lenses.

The other way of looking at life is with consideration toward eternity. It is not limited by earth time or circumstances that come and go. Why? Because eternity has no beginning, middle, or end. It just *is*—eternal. In order to view life from that perspective, it must be seen through Biblical-World-View lenses.

Seeing life here through earth-based world-view lenses requires no consideration of what takes place after death. The hereafter doesn't even enter into the vista of temporal/earth-restricted perception. No faith (in anything or anybody) is necessary. Hope in and of itself is only appropriated in regards to life as it is, while on earth. Life is what it is, so to speak.

A Biblical-World-View incorporates not only consideration for what happens after death, it also factors in the Bible as the main source of light, both now and later.

> *"For with you is the fountain of life; in your light do we see light."*
>
> ~Ps. 36:9

> *"Your word is a lamp to my feet and a light to my path."*
> ~Ps. 119:105

In order to see—really see—the kingdom of God, life must be viewed through the prism of Scripture. At least that's how I see it.

> *"And without faith it is impossible to please him, for whoever would draw near to God must believe that he exists and that he rewards those who *seek him."*
>
> ~Heb. 11:6

*diligently seek him (KJV)

17

That right there is a profound portion of Scripture. The phrase "it is impossible to please" is a mind blower of sorts. It jumps directly off the page whenever I read it, as if it's written in **EXTRA-LARGE** type. I see it as being the key wording in that verse. However, there are three other phrases that interact with it:

- "...without faith"
- "...must believe that he exists"
- "...rewards those who *seek him"

I may (or may not) sort out those first two phrases later. For now, heading into the topic at hand—questing—I'll begin by considering what it means to seek something (or someone) with diligence. To do so creates a direct link to the language of Mt. 6:33. In that verse, Jesus places a charge upon *all* those who would follow Him:

> *"But seek first the kingdom of God and His righteousness, and all these things will be added to you."*

If/When you read that verse in its context, you'll see what "these things" are. But, my focus here isn't on "these things," rather, it's on two key words in specific, "seek first."

When the "seek him" (diligently) of Heb. 11:6 and "seek first" in Mt. 6:33 are considered together, a pathway of questing begins to open up. That's where this trek begins...

There is a term used in the legal profession that applies here. It is, *due diligence.* Here's what it means:

Due diligence is a legal phrase that describes the act of making an appropriate level of investigation when considering a decision, being appropriately cautious. *Due diligence* often refers to the process of vetting a business that is for sale, looking at its assets and liabilities. *Due diligence* is also used to mean taking the necessary precautions to avoid the commission of an offense. The phrase *due diligence* is a combination of the words *due,* derived from the Latin word *debere* which means to owe, and *diligence,* derived from the

Latin word *diligentia,* which means **carefulness or attentiveness**. The term *due diligence* has been in use in a legal sense since the mid-1400s.

The portion of the definition that applies to this narrative is that of "carefulness or attentiveness." Seeking the kingdom of God as first priority (Mt. 6:33) and seeking Him (Heb. 11:6) both require that "due diligence" be used in regards to careful consideration, practical processing, and appropriate application.

Jesus said, "seek first the kingdom of God and His righteousness…" (Mt. 6:33) Christ said that to His followers in real time. But, by extension, He still says that to those who follow Him now. That text is the only place in all of Scripture where He establishes the first thing which is to be at the very top of a spiritual "to-do" list.

"Jesus never declared 'Seek first…' about any pursuit or purpose except for the Kingdom of God. The Kingdom was the central message of His teaching and ministry on earth, and that of His disciples." (Jack Taylor)

In regards to being pro-active with that directive, He spoke the Beatitudes and the Sermon on the Mount as guidelines for living a lifestyle based on what He considered as essential data for believers. The Beatitudes are the startup steps, and the Sermon on the Mount is the complete protocol for how Kingdom living is designed to function. More on that later. (See Mt. 5, 6, and 7).

For me personally, the challenge of such a calling has become much more important in the last decade than it has ever been—especially over the last five years or so.

Oswald Chambers sees this topic much as I do. There are others who do so well. Perhaps you are (or will become) one of them.

"When we first read the statements of Jesus, they seem wonderfully simple and unstartling, and they sink unnoticed into our subconscious minds. For instance, the Beatitudes initially seem to be merely soothing and beautiful precepts for overly spiritual and seemingly useless people, but of very

little practical use in the rigid, fast-paced workdays of the world in which we live. We soon find, however, that the Beatitudes contain the "dynamite" of the Holy Spirit. And they "explode" when the circumstances of our lives cause them to do so. When the Holy Spirit brings to our remembrance one of the Beatitudes, we say, "What a startling statement that is!" Then we must decide whether or not we will accept the tremendous spiritual upheaval that will be produced in our circumstances if we obey His words. That is the way the Spirit of God works. We do not need to be born again to apply the Sermon on the Mount literally. The literal interpretation of the Sermon on the Mount is as easy as child's play. But the interpretation by the Spirit of God as He applies our Lord's statements to our circumstances is the strict and difficult work of a saint.

The teachings of Jesus are all out of proportion when compared to our natural way of looking at things, and they come to us initially with astonishing discomfort. We gradually have to conform our walk and conversation to the precepts of Jesus Christ as the Holy Spirit applies them to our circumstances. The Sermon on the Mount is not a set of rules and regulations— it is a picture of the life we will live when the Holy Spirit is having His unhindered way with us."

~Oswald Chambers

"The two most important things Jesus ever spoke, the Lord's Prayer and the Beatitudes, both began with the kingdom of God. And the most important thing he said in the Sermon on the Mount was: *"Seek first ye the kingdom of God,...and all these things shall be added unto you"* (Mt. 6:33). So first and last and between times the emphasis is on the kingdom. And not a marginal emphasis, but the organizing emphasis upon which everything revolved and from which everything gets its meaning. We have become so accustomed to the insane

un-Kingdom was of life that we are afraid of the sanity of the Kingdom. This is particularly true of the Sermon on the Mount which contains many, if not most of the laws, the principles, and the attitudes of the kingdom of God. As we unfold the laws, principles, and attitudes of the kingdom of God as seen in the Sermon on the Mount, I believe we will be astonished at the sheer sanity of the Kingdom."

~E. Stanley Jones

In his book entitled, *The Kingdom: The Emerging Rule Of Christ Among Men,* George Dana Boardman presents profound and insightful detailed data that is well worth consideration. One of the key aspects he addresses is the distinction between the Kingdom and the church. I'm including his narrative in full from the manuscript's introduction. It's important in the development of this chapter.

"Two words occur in the New Testament so frequently that they largely characterize it, and almost dominate it.

Basileia—The first of these two words translates as "Kingdom." This word as a religious term occurs one hundred and forty times and nine times in the Gospels; eight times in the Acts of the Apostles ; fourteen times in the Letters of Paul; twice in the Letter to the Hebrews; once in the General Letter of James; once in the Second General Letter of Peter; five times in the Revelation.

Ecclesia—The second of these two words translates as "Church." The word as a religious term occurs one hundred and eleven times: three times in the First Gospel; twenty times in the Acts of the Apostles; sixty-two times in the Letters of Paul; twice in the Letter to the Hebrews; once in the Letter of James; three times in the Third Letter of John; twenty times in the Revelation.

The two words used Discriminatingly. Believing that

when the sacred writers used these two words, "Basileia"*or "Kingdom,"* and "Ecclesia" or "Church," they used them discriminatingly, a careful study of them in their chronological order and in their relative frequency yields lessons which are very suggestive. For example, thus:

Basileia the Christly word: *Ecclesia* the Apostolic word.— The word "Basileia" or "Kingdom" is characteristic of the Gospels, occurring one hundred and nine times out of the one hundred and forty; the word "Ecclesia"* or "Church" is characteristic of the Acts and the Letters, occurring one hundred and eight times out of the one hundred and eleven; or, to put it in another way, *Basileia* is the Christly word, *Ecclesia* is the Apostolic word.

Basileia is Divine: *Ecclesia* is Human.—Again, in "Basileia"; "Kingdom" the Divine or Kingly element prevails—it is the Reign of God; in "Ecclesia"; "Church" the human or social element prevails—it is a congregation of Christians. Or to put it in another form: in *Basileia* Christianity appears as a spiritual organism—"Righteousness, and peace, and joy in the Holy Spirit"; in *Ecclesia,* Christianity appears as an institutional organization—"The ecclesia which was in Jerusalem."*

Basileia is God's End: *Ecclesia* is God's Means,—Once more and in sum, *Basileia* or Kingdom is God's end—the goal of Christianity; *Ecclesia* or Church is God's means—the method of Christianity. Thus the Kingdom descends in order that the Church may ascend.

Accordingly, as "Kingdom" precedes "Church," both chronologically and logically, our subject naturally cleaves into two parts—the Christian Kingdom and the Christian Church."

Quoting from *The Unshakeable Kingdom And The Unchanging Person,* E. Stanley Jones insights addresses a situation he was living in, that today resounds prophetically

"God's kingdom must be by its very nature a total kingdom, for God is not a half-god ruling over a half-realm, ruling

over the personal but not over the social, or ruling over the social and not over the personal. Nor must he be a god who fits into the unexplained facts of nature and not into the total facts of nature, its regularity as well as its unexplained mysteries. He must be totally present or totally absent and hence totally irrelevant. He must be God and not a mere half-god. And his kingdom must be totally present and totally relevant or totally nothing and hence totally irrelevant. There is no middle ground. You cannot tuck God into the unexplained gaps in nature, for those unexplained gaps in nature have a way of being filled up and then where is God? He must be God of all or not God at all. And his kingdom must be a total kingdom or no kingdom."

Over the centuries, humankind has considered the kingdom in a modified form, as a spiritual refuge into which they could run and be safe now or as a place of reward in heaven; they didn't reject it—they reduced it.

And in reducing it they rendered it innocuous now. It wasn't the kingdom, God's total answer to man's total need. It wasn't God's total plane and program for life, all life, now, but a reward thrown in at the end.

And, now life has become so physically dynamic, so mentally and emotionally free, and so morally irresponsible that it is bursting at the seams; it is going to pieces at the very moment of our greatest triumph in so many fields—in every field except the field of living. We know everything about life except how to live it. We need nothing so desperately as we need something to bring life into total unity and coherence and meaning and goal. We have become ripe—dead ripe—for a rediscovery of the kingdom of God.

So for the Church to be relevant the answer is simple: Discover the kingdom, surrender to the kingdom, make the kingdom your life loyalty and your life program; then in everything and everywhere you will be relevant. For the kingdom

of God is relevance—ultimate and final relevance and when you have it, and it has you, then you are relevance itself."

"The Kingdom concept as a whole has been lost to contemporary human culture, especially in the Western world. In his attempt to create the kingdom of heaven on earth, man has opted to design his own forms of government. But his experiments continue to fail: evil kingdoms, empires, dictators, communism, socialism, democracy…and the list goes on. The desire for righteous government burns in the heart of every human. All of us are seeking the Kingdom even if we all don't realize it."

~Myles Munroe

"When we obey the laws of the kingdom of God we are obeying the laws of our own being. It is the natural way to live."

~E. Stanley Jones

I believe Jones is saying that humanity was created (designed) to function based on the principles, precepts, and laws of God's kingdom. Since God's kingdom was fashioned "before the foundation of the earth" (Eph. 1:3-14), it is to be understood as existing outside of earth time. It is eternal, without beginning, middle, or end. According to scripture, the very essence of the Kingdom—its *"eternal otherness"*—has been placed in the hearts of every human being who has ever lived, is living now, or will live in the future.

"He has made everything beautiful in its time. Also, he has put eternity into man's heart…"

~Ecc. 3:11a

Keep in mind that when Jesus said, *"the kingdom of God is within you"* (Lu. 17:21), he was speaking to the Pharisees, not to his disciples.

24

Therefore, the Kingdom is available to any and all who will enter into it—by receiving Christ Jesus as Lord and Savior, and then living out their lives in yielded obedience to the Holy Ghost.

Yielded obedience is the very root of worship. Worship is obedient service manifesting through self-sacrifice. (Wayne-Speak)

See Rom. 12:1, 2 (MSG and Col. 3:17)

Based on the language of Scripture, there is an aspect of worship contained in the definition of the word *seek*. As I see it, any consideration of seeking for the kingdom of God should not be undertaken without the inclusion of worship. And, to me, such an inclusion begins with the first commandment declaration in Deut. 5:7 which says, "You shall have no other gods *before Me."

*The NASB (and other translations) use the word *besides* instead of *before*. Doing so broadens the meaning and widens the perspective on what that text says.

Here at the beginning of this priority pathway, entering the detailed coordinates of that verse into our navigation system (GOSPEL POSITIONING SYSTEM) will help to set our course in place.

Here they are:

Coordinate #1

Our first coordinate is to place worship of God as our singular Sovereign. He is to be our "go to" destination. (Deut. 5:7)

In that text, the word *gods* is in lower case. The *g* isn't capitalized as in the singular *God*. So, any and all other deities are to be understood as subordinate to the One True God (Isa. 43:11/Jn. 17:3/1 Cor. 8:6/1 Tim. 1:17; 2:5). They are lesser gods (Ps. 135:16). It is also plural in its usage, meaning there is a multiplicity of them. This is a very important concept to consider. The narrative isn't disavowing the presence of other gods. No, it is acknowledging them. The directive is saying that whatever other gods there are, they are not to be worshipped over, above, or "besides" Jehovah— the Sovereign Creator of the universe (Ps. 146:6).

Keep in mind that I'm addressing the subject of worship because

it should be included in any consideration of seeking the kingdom of God.

The seeking (in and of itself) carries with it a desire to elevate (exalt) the Father, Son, and Holy Ghost with adoration and our faithful obedient service. Therefore the component of worship is directly linked with Kingdom seeking.

> "The Kingdom is the ultimate, absolute reality because it has its existence and identity in Him. We must realize that what is true of the King is also true of His Kingdom. The two are inseparable. To think of One is to think of the other; to seek One is to seek the other. When we seek Jesus, we seek His Kingdom, which is the Kingdom of the Father. When we find the Kingdom, we find Jesus and His omnipresent reign."
>
> ~Jack Taylor

FINDING THE KINGDOM

In Mt. 6:33, the Greek word for *seek is zeteo*, meaning to worship God; to endeavor; find out about; desire, enquire.

In Heb. 11:6 it is *ekzeteo*, meaning to search out, investigate, crave, demand, worship.

Based on that foundational language, clearly both aspects of seeking contain a worship component. Therefore, seeking can be understood as an act of worship. With that in mind, ponder this rendering of Mt. 6:33:

As an act of worship, seek first the kingdom of God...

Framed in that fashion, establishing a clear definition of worship becomes an essential part of Kingdom seeking. In other words, seeking as an act of worship first requires a basic Biblical understanding of what worship is.

Coordinate #2:

Position God as the *only* object of worship. To do so is to place

ourselves in submission to His rule (His Word, His will, and His ways). That can only be achieved through obedience to His purposes and plans. Such obedience is [in fact] worship in essence.

Keep my working definition of worship in mind as we continue our Kingdom sojourn:

Worship is obedient service manifesting through self-sacrifice.

"Developing a Kingdom mind-set begins with learning the nature of the Kingdom: a Kingdom requires a sovereign ruler; those who are ruled; and rules." (Jack Taylor)

In regards to worship and obedience, here are two examples from Scripture:

From the Old Testament, consider Gen. 22:1-5:

> *"After these things God tested Abraham and said to him, "Abraham!" And he said, "Here I am." He said, "Take your son, your only son Isaac, whom you love, and go to the land of Moriah, and offer him there as a burnt offering on one of the mountains of which I shall tell you." So Abraham rose early in the morning, saddled his donkey, and took two of his young men with him, and his son Isaac. And he cut the wood for the burnt offering and arose and went to the place of which God had told him. On the third day Abraham lifted up his eyes and saw the place from afar. Then Abraham said to his young men, "Stay here with the donkey; I and the boy will go over there and worship and come again to you."*

There is an approach that can be used in the study of Scripture. It's called the principle of first usage (or first mention). The essence of the concept is this: The first time a word appears in the Bible can be considered as offering the basic meaning of the word. Thereafter, all the other meanings and usages are established based on that first usage.

Gen. 22:5 is the first place in Scripture where the word *worship* is found. In that context, this is its meaning:

To depress; prostrate (in homage to royalty or God); to bow, crouch, fall down, humbly beseech, show reverence, make to stoop.

From the New Testament, consider Rom. 12:1, 2 (MSG)

"So here's what I want you to do, God helping you: Take your everyday, ordinary life—your sleeping, eating, going-to-work, and walking-around life—and place it before God as an offering. Embracing what God does for you is the best thing you can do for him. Don't become so well-adjusted to your culture that you fit into it without even thinking. Instead, fix your attention on God. You'll be changed from the inside out. Readily recognize what he wants from you, and quickly respond to it. Unlike the culture around you, always dragging you down to its level of immaturity, God brings the best out of you, develops well-formed maturity in you."

For me personally, those are the two most important instructive examples of obedient worship in Scripture. However, there is one other verse that is perhaps the most meaningful:

"And whatever you do, in word or deed, do everything in the name of the Lord Jesus, giving thanks to God the Father through him."

~Col. 3:17

That text speaks to consecration, obedience, and worship like no other I know. It is a "life verse" for me. I carry it deep in my soul.

NOTE: I'll explore Consecration, Obedience, and Worship in a later chapter as this narrative develops.

With those three portions of Scripture in mind (Gen. 22:1-5 / Rom. 12:1, 2 / Col. 3:17), ponder the dynamics of Jn. 4:23 which states *"… the hour is coming, and is now here, when the true worshipers will worship the Father in spirit and truth, for the Father is seeking such people to worship him."*

Take note of the following aspects of that verse: God is seeking for "true worshippers."

The phrase "true worshippers" implies that there are also false

28

worshippers. There can't be one without the other. That being the case, approach the concept this way:

All people ever born, living now, or yet to be born are [in fact] worshippers of something or somebody. They are either true in their worship, or false, depending on to whom or to what their worship is given. That is exactly what Deut. 5:7 is addressing. A person's worship is given either to The One True God, or to lesser god(s).

Therefore, from among all worshippers, God is seeking for a specific kind—those who will worship Him—first and foremost, with singular focus and intention. Such a focused worship is what is presented in the Rom. 12:1, 2 passage.

The mutual seeking taking place between God and "true worshippers" is the main point of Jn. 4:23. The subordinate portion of that text is that of "spirit and truth." It is my personal observation that the contemporary perspective most often addressed is the "spirit and truth" aspect, with far less attention being given to the "true worshippers" concept. When that occurs, attention is drawn away from the commandment of Deut. 5:7, which sets the stage for idolatry to begin to take hold in the lives of worshippers. They, in turn, become false worshippers, instead of true worshippers. And that is, in essence, what idolatry is.

> *"The idols of the nations are silver and gold, the work of human hands. They have mouths, but do not speak; they have eyes, but do not see; they have ears, but do not hear, nor is there any breath in their mouths. Those who make them become like them, so do all who trust in them."*
>
> ~Ps. 135:15-18

> *"Do you not know that if you present yourselves to anyone as obedient slaves, you are slaves of the one whom you obey, either of sin, which leads to death, or of obedience, which leads to righteousness?"*
>
> ~Rom. 6:16

Very briefly, I'll comment on the "spirit , truth" aspect, just to give it some passing consideration:

The word *spirit* in context means a current of air; breath; our vital principle or mental disposition. The whole of our being.

The word *truth* in context means verity; something not concealed. What we believe about what we believe.

Both those words (in their contexts) are certainly important. However, as I've already stated, the "true worshippers" concept deserves much more attention than it is customarily given currently in our lives and lifestyles. Simply stated, the "spirit , truth" components are to follow after the "true worshippers" aspect. The *Who* and *what* of our worship determines the *how*, not the other way 'round.

God Himself is seeking for seekers.

John 4:23 in the KJV uses the word *seeketh* (KJV). It's the same word as in Heb. 11:6. You could read the verse this way:

The Father is seeking *worshippers* who are seeking *Him* in spirit and truth.

That is to say, He is seeking Kingdom seekers, which is exactly what Jesus said should be the first priority for *all* those who follow Him (Mt. 6:33). Such seeking contains (includes/incorporates) worship as part of a dynamic process. Thus, Kingdom seekers become true worshippers (or vice versa) in a Biblical sense. Therefore, what Jesus said was important to Him is [in fact] important to the Father. And, the Holy Spirit is the force behind the source of the seeking (See Acts 1:8).

The dynamic process of Acts 1:8 is as follows:

Presence precedes Power / Power prompts Witness / Witness proclaims Testimony / Testimony produces Revival

Our second coordinate setting is obedient service to the "One True God" (Isa. 46:1-13), manifesting through self-sacrifice (Gen. 22:5 / Rom. 12:1, 2 / Col. 3:17).

Developing A Kingdom Mindset

Questing for the kingdom of God is not geographical (Jn. 18:36a). The physical location is not the destination. Followers of Christ are charged with bringing the Kingdom above down to earth (Mt. 6:10). That has more to do with learning how the Kingdom functions there, in order to then bring it to where we live here—on earth as it is in heaven. Mental ascension, cognitive comprehension, and the acquisition of awareness are all key components of such a journey. Learning to understand, relate to, and function in God's kingdom is most likely how such a spiritual sojourn is best undertaken. It's an inside-out process. An internal locating of the Kingdom, resident in our lives, is essential in order for it to then manifest externally (Lu. 17:20, 21).

The basic definition of *repentance* is to change our way of thinking. For the most part, we tend to think of repentance related only to issues of conviction, and confession of sin. That isn't an incorrect usage of the term as such. It is however, incomplete. Thinking only with a temporal (earthly) perspective will not lead us to a place of clarity in regards to insights and inter-actions in the kingdom of God. A changed lifestyle requires a certain style of life.

Ponder these passages:

> *"I appeal to you therefore, brothers, by the mercies of God, to present your bodies as a living sacrifice, holy and acceptable to God, which is your spiritual worship. Do not be conformed to this world, but be *transformed by the *renewal of your mind, that by testing you may discern what is the will of God, what is good and acceptable and perfect."*
>
> ~Rom. 12:1, 2

*Transformed: Changed; transfigure; metamorphose. From a word meaning to refashion.

**Renewal (renewing / KJV) meaning renovation.

31

> *"[If] then you have been raised with Christ, seek the things that are above, where Christ is, seated at the right hand of God. Set your minds on things that are above, not on things that are on earth. For you have died, and your life is hidden with Christ in God. When Christ who is your life appears, then you also will appear with him in glory."*
>
> ~Col. 3:1-4

*[If] is a conditional word. It means that everything that's stated in that passages applies directly to those who are "hidden with Christ in God."

Also, the word *minds* is *affection* in the KJV. It means to exercise the mind; to be (mentally) disposed (more or less in a certain direction); to interest oneself in (with concern or obedience).

Quoting Jack Taylor: "I've discovered that an expanded understanding of the kingdom must involve a continual readiness on our part to change our minds about many things, as well as to accept kingdom revelation that leads us above our previous conceptions. Developing a kingdom mind-set begins wit learning the nature of the kingdom. The word *kingdom* itself begs definition, especially in a democratic society where the term is seldom used and even less understood. And kingdom on earth includes three things: a King or queen, kingdom citizens, and the principles that characterize the relationship between the two. Or, to put it succinctly: a sovereign ruler; those who are ruled; and "rules."

There are three ways of responding to The Kingdom:

- From outside of it—disinterested, misinformed, dismissive, unaware.
- From inside of it—passively planted, non-participator, tentative, and statically stationary. In it, yes, but not involved.
- From inside of it—adventurous, explorative, pro-actively participatory, and fluidly flowing.

The first one excludes you from any and all involvement altogether. The second two identify and involve you as a Kingdom

citizen (1 Peter 2:9). But, only the third one provides full access and full value to being in it.

Pondering Priorities

Redemption of the spiritual kind is readily available (Jn. 3:16), but it can be hard to appropriate (Phil. 3:7-10). It takes surrendering to The Creator of the universe, accepting His Son (as the Savior of humankind), and obediently yielding to the Holy Ghost. Thereafter, a salvific life is to be lived by filling it up with as many redemptive components as possible. That process has a name—it's called *sanctification.*

Acquiring such redemptive components requires a Kingdom focus that far too few folks seem to care much about these daze (Mt. 6:33).

Now, before you start shoutin' me down, be advised that I don't make such public assessments as that every day. But, today I am. (See Col. 3:1-4 (MSG.)

*"But whatever gain I had, I counted as loss for the sake of Christ. Indeed, I count everything as loss because of the surpassing worth of knowing Christ Jesus my Lord. For his sake I have suffered the loss of all things and count them as *rubbish, in order that I may gain Christ and be found in him, not having a righteousness of my own that comes from the law, but that which comes through faith in Christ, the righteousness from God that depends on faith— that I may know him and the power of his resurrection, and may share his sufferings, becoming like him in his death, that by any means possible I may attain the resurrection from the dead. Not that I have already obtained this or am already perfect, but I press on to make it my own, because Christ Jesus has made me his own. Brothers, I do not consider that I have made it my own. But one thing I do: forgetting what lies behind and straining forward to what lies*

ahead, I press on toward the goal for the prize of the upward call of God in Christ Jesus."

~Phil. 3:7-14

Rubbish is rendered as *dung* in the KJV. Paul was just sayin'... When you walk in a calling, even scars are sacred.

Section Two
THE ENTRANCE

ENTERING IN (ACCESS GRANTED)

T he point of entry into the kingdom of God is through the act of redemption:

> *"Jesus said to him, 'I am the way, and the truth, and the life. No one comes to the Father except through me.'"*
>
> ~Jn. 14:6

> *"And there is salvation in no one else, for there is no other name under heaven given among men by which we must be saved."*
>
> ~Acts 4:12

Those who accept Christ Jesus as their Lord, and Savior are delivered and transferred:

> *"He has delivered us from the domain of darkness and transferred us to the kingdom of his beloved Son, in whom we have redemption, the forgiveness of sins."*
>
> ~Col. 1:13-15

35

The words *delivered* and *transferred* are both past tense.

> *"...for at one time you were darkness, but now you are light in*
> *the Lord. Walk as children of light."*
>
> ~Eph. 5:8

That verse says those who are "hidden with Christ in God" (Col. 3:1-4) are "children of light." They are not becoming, they already are. (See Eph. 2:14, 15)

The redeemed in and of the Lord are given specific guidelines to follow (practice) which provide an opened entranceway into the kingdom:

> *"For this very reason, make every effort to supplement your faith*
> *with virtue, and virtue with knowledge, and knowledge with*
> *self-control, and self-control with steadfastness, and steadfast-*
> *ness with godliness, and godliness with brotherly affection, and*
> *brotherly affection with love. For if these qualities are yours and*
> *are increasing, they keep you from being ineffective or unfruitful*
> *in the knowledge of our Lord Jesus Christ. For whoever lacks*
> *these qualities is so nearsighted that he is blind, having forgotten*
> *that he was cleansed from his former sins. Therefore, brothers,*
> *be all the more diligent to confirm your calling and election,*
> *for if you practice these qualities you will never fall. For in this*
> *way there will be richly provided for you an entrance into the*
> *eternal kingdom of our Lord and Savior Jesus Christ."*
>
> ~2 Peter 1:5-11

From Grace To Hope To Faith

The subject of grace is vast. It is considerably deeper and wider than we really understand. That being said, the comments that follow are intended as a sort of primer regarding the shape and substance of it. I'll begin with the working definition for grace that I've been using the last decade or thereabouts.

"Grace is the favor of God's empowering presence, enabling me to be who He created me to be, so I can do what He calls me to do."

~J. Ryle

Attempting to limit the scope of grace is an impossible task. However, for the sake of time and clarity of content, I'll address only two aspects of it:

1. Grace is redemptive in gift form
2. Grace is also receivable by request or solicitation

The gift of grace (Eph. 2:8) provides the entrance way into God's kingdom. The only requirement on our part is to receive it as the gift that it is. That is to say, it's ours if we will take it. Understood in that way, grace is redemptive.

It is also available directly through acquisition, by way of request (Heb. 4:16). Understood in that way, grace is receivable (renewable).

The unfolding of that process enables us to move deeper and further into the kingdom of God. Simply stated, it presents like this:

Grace flows directly from the throne of God by request (Heb. 4:16). From there it streams out into hope (2 Thess. 2:16, 17). Then, it manifests as faith (Heb. 11:1)

Grace imparted to us through our request is transformed into hope. And, hope is then manifested as faith. From there, we walk (live out) our faith, which in turn cycles us directly back to grace (Rom. 5:1, 2). I call that the Cycle of Hope.

The Dynamics of the Cycle of Hope:
- Hope flows out of grace (2 Thess. 2:16)
- Renewed/Increased hope manifests as faith (Heb. 11:1)
- Faith (in turn) introduces us to grace (Rom. 5:1, 2)

And the cycle continues…

THEOLOGY DEFINED: The study of religious faith, practice, and experience; the study of God and of God's relation to the world.

"...love the Lord with all your heart, soul, *mind, and strength"

> ~Mr. 12:30 (NASB)

"...loving Him with all passion and *intelligence and energy..."

> ~Mr. 12:30 (MSG)

*Mind: Deep thought; the faculty (of mind or disposition); to exercise the imagination; to gain understanding.

HOPE DEFINED: Confident expectation

"If we have hope in Christ in this life [only], we are of all men most to be pitied."

> ~1 Cor. 15:19 (NASB) with emphasis

"If all we get out of Christ is a little inspiration for a [a few short years], we're a pretty sorry lot."

> ~1 Cor. 15:19 (MSG) with emphasis

"For the grace of God has appeared, bringing salvation to all men, instructing us to deny ungodliness and worldly desires and to live sensibly, righteously and godly in the present age, looking for the blessed hope and the appearing of the glory of our great God and Savior, Christ Jesus..."

> ~Titus 2:11-13

Where does hope come from?

2 Thess. 2:16 says in part, "God our Father has given us eternal comfort and good hope by grace..."

"Therefore, prepare your minds for action, keep sober in spirit, fix your hope completely on grace..."

> ~1 Peter 1:13

FAITH DEFINED: A way of walking

"Faith is the substance of things hoped for, the evidence of things not seen."

~Heb. 11:1

Part of what faith does: "...faith introduces us to grace...." (Rom. 5:1, 2)

"Grace is the favor of God's empowering presence, enabling me to be who He created me to be, so I can do what He calls me to do."

~J. Ryle

"Cheap grace is the grace we bestow on ourselves. Cheap grace is the preaching of forgiveness without requiring repentance, baptism without church discipline, Communion without confession.... Cheap grace is grace without discipleship, grace without the cross, grace without Jesus Christ, living and incarnate."

Dietrich Bonhoeffer
See also Rom. 6 and note verse 16

Where does grace come from?
- 1st Work of Grace: "By grace are we saved through faith, it is a gift from God...." (Eph. 2:8)
- 2nd Work of Grace: "Therefore let us draw near with confidence to the throne of grace, so that we may receive mercy and find grace to help in time of need." (Heb. 4:16 (NASB)

Closing:
- Hope flows out of grace (2 Thess. 2:16, 17)
- Renewed hope manifests as faith (Heb. 11:1)
- Faith (in turn) introduces us to grace (Rom. 5:1, 2)

And the cycle continues...

Redemptive Components (The Process Of Consecration)

To me, the following passage is one of the most important and meaningful in the entire Bible (especially v.17). I'm sharing it in four translations, just so you can wrap yourself in the light that it sheds forth.

Let the peace of Christ keep you in tune with each other, in step with each other. None of this going off and doing your own thing. And cultivate thankfulness. Let the Word of Christ—the Message—have the run of the house. Give it plenty of room in your lives. Instruct and direct one another using good common sense. And sing, sing your hearts out to God!
~Colossians 3:15-17 (MSG)

Let your heart be always guided by the peace of the Anointed One, who called you to peace as part of his one body. And always be thankful. Let the word of Christ live in you richly, flooding you with all wisdom. Apply the Scriptures as you teach and instruct one another with the Psalms, and with festive praises, and with prophetic songs given to you spontaneously by the Spirit, so sing to God with all your hearts!
~Colossians 3:15-17 (TPT)

Let every activity of your lives and every word that comes from your lips be drenched with the beauty of our Lord Jesus, the Anointed One. And bring your constant praise to God the Father because of what Christ has done for you!
~Colossians 3:15-17 (Phillips)

Let the peace of Christ rule in your hearts, remembering that as members of the same body you are called to live in harmony, and never forget to be thankful for what God has done for you. Let Christ's teaching live in your hearts, making you rich in

the true wisdom. Teach and help one another along the right road with your psalms and hymns and Christian songs, singing God's praises with joyful hearts. And whatever you may have to do, do everything in the name of the Lord Jesus, thanking God the Father through him.

~Colossians 3:15-17

"And let the peace of Christ rule in your hearts, to which indeed you were called in one body. And be thankful. Let the word of Christ dwell in you richly, teaching and admonishing one another in all wisdom, singing psalms and hymns and spiritual songs, with thankfulness in your hearts to God. And whatever you do, in word or deed, do everything in the name of the Lord Jesus, giving thanks to God the Father through him."

The text tells us to give free reign to the peace of Christ in our lives as His followers. That's because we've been called (appointed) to do so. It also says that thanksgiving should be a proactive condition in which we live. Further, it directs us to allow the Word of God to have permanent residence in us which can enable us to teach and admonish one another in wisdom while cultivating the gift of music (in psalms, hymns, and spiritual songs). Each of those aspects of spirituality are deserving of much consideration and application. Then the passage closes by stating one of the most profound Biblical directives in Scripture:

"Whatever you do in word or deed, do all in the name of the Lord Jesus, giving thanks through Him to God the Father."

~Col. 3:17 (NASB)

That's the focus of what I'm going to address next.

To begin, this is my working definition for *consecration*: Consecration is the setting apart of any person, place, or thing for acts of holy service.

41

Without commitment to the principle and practice of consecration, it's impossible to fully implement what Colossians 3:17 says we are to do as believers. Here's what I mean by making that statement:

For without first being willing to live a lifestyle which is based on accomplishing acts of holy service, it is impossible to do so. Put simply, surrendering your life to Christ is at its basic level an act of consecration in and of itself. However you prayed your first prayer of confession and repentance, regardless of whether you knew it or not, you were performing your first formative act in the process of consecrating your life to Kingdom service. You were asking the Lord to take your life and set it apart for His service in any way He wanted that to take place. And that is [in fact] consecration. By doing so, you entered into a process which is meant to carry you along the "highway of holiness" (Isa. 35:8a / KJV) which leads all the way up to Zion.

> *"How enriched are they who find their strength in the Lord; within their hearts are the highways of holiness! Even when their paths wind through the dark valley of tears, they dig deep to find a pleasant pool where others find only pain. He gives to them a brook of blessing filled from the rain of an outpouring. They grow stronger and stronger with every step forward, and the God of all gods will appear before them in Zion."*
> ~Ps. 84:5-7 (TPT)

The so-called "Sinners Prayer" is therefore an act of consecration, regardless of what words are used or whether or not a full understanding was taking place at the moment. Giving one's life to God, through Christ Jesus, prompted and enabled by the Holy Ghost, is without a doubt a consecrated act. However, the original act only *begins* the process.

In other words, the act provides an entrance on to the pathway that followers of Christ are called to walk along till they die or

till Jesus returns for His own. At least that's how I understand the principle and practice was designed to function.

Having said all that, I'm going to unpack how I see the process of consecration taking place using some key Scriptural examples. In order to do that, I need to clarify a language issue that can be confusing without some clear and concise consideration:

In the KJV (and some other translations), the word *consecration* is presented as being interchangeable with the word *sanctification.* That is misleading, as I understand those two terms. As I've already mentioned, consecration begins (or requires) a setting apart. That's our job. In other words, the process is one we have to initiate ourselves. Sanctification is—according to Scripture—the work of the Holy Ghost on our behalf. (See 1 Thess. 4:3 / 1 Peter 1:2 / Rom. 15:16 / Jude 1.)

Here's perhaps the best example from the Word to explain what I'm saying:

> *"And Joshua said unto the people, 'Sanctify yourselves: for tomorrow the Lord will do wonders among you.'"*
> ~Josh.3:5 (KJV)

The use of the word *sanctify* in that verse is misleading since the New Testament clearly states that the Holy Ghost is responsible for any sanctifying work which takes place in the life of a believer. A better rendering of it would be,:

> *"Then Joshua said to the people, 'Consecrate yourselves, for tomorrow the Lord will do wonders among you.'"*
> ~Josh.3:5 (NASB)

See the difference? Consecration is our job, and sanctification is that of the Spirit.

Before I continue, I need to provide a disclaimer of sorts.

It is possible for someone to consecrate another person, place,

or thing for acts of holy service other than themselves. However, in order to do so, the person doing that has to have the authority to carry out such an act. And, the person, place, or thing has to be established through the act of consecration—for the service of consecration—by carrying out the things which validate the act itself. Once the person with authority has released consecration, they no longer bear the personal responsibility of bringing it to pass. That becomes the charge of others to fulfill. An example of that is found in Jeremiah 1:5 which says: *"Before I formed you in the womb I knew you, and before you were born I consecrated you; I have appointed you a prophet to the nations."* (NASB)

Here we see that Jehovah has done the consecrating. Thereafter, it is Jeremiah's task to walk it out. Said another way, God set him apart, and it became his assignment to live it out in a life of consecrated service.

There's another aspect of the process of consecration which has to do with how and when the process itself is to be carried out. I'll show you what I mean by opening up Joshua 3:5 a little more in order to see it from another angle than just the words of the page.

To catch the dynamic of what that verse says, it needs to be considered from an active real-time perspective:

Joshua tells the people to consecrate themselves based on what Jehovah is about to do in their midst. In other words, they are to prepare for what's about to happen prior to the event taking place. The best way to see that unfolding is to read the text like this:

"Consecrate yourselves [TODAY], for tomorrow the Lord will do wonders among you."

The *act* of consecration is to be addressed and set in motion before the need to *serve* consecrated becomes necessary. To not do so can result in missing the opportunity to be directly involved in what's going to take place, because the prerequisite setting apart hasn't happened.

I know this can get confusing to sort through, so I'll provide another example from a practical viewpoint to help you see what I'm saying.

Let's suppose I purpose to invite a few friends on an all-expenses paid trip to somewhere wonderful. So, I have them all meet me for dinner where everyone covers their own meal. Before we finish to head home, I tell them about my surprise "gift." After they all get over the shock of the news, I tell them there are just two things they are required to do:

1. Go home and sort out time away from work and all their daily responsibilities.
2. Show up at the airport early enough to make certain they won't miss the flight.

Then I tell them that if they don't take care of point #1 it will likely make it impossible for them to join us. And, if they don't attend to point #2, those who are have checked in at the boarding gate will *leave without them*!

That, friend(s), is how the process of consecration is designed to work. You have to take care of everything that is needed for a set-apart life *before* "any participation begins" to take place. If not, it is possible that you'll be aware that something wonderful is taking place. You may even be able to see it unfolding. However, you might not be able to take part in any aspect of the action. Why? Because you didn't consecrate yourself prior to the need for consecration to be in place.

Selah (pause, ponder)

Now look at (meaning *read*) 2 Chronicles 29 for a Biblically-based scene to unfold regarding the consecration process. This is important to conveying this story: You'll need the entire chapter for context and outcome. However, I'll just focus on verses 31-36 with a brief overview.

The short version presented in 2 Chronicles 20:31-36 goes like this:

A service (celebration/holy convocation) is taking place. Due

to unexpected circumstances, those who needed to be prepared to serve (the priests) had not consecrated themselves properly. However, the musicians who had come to serve in their capacity as musicians had [in fact] set themselves apart for holy service *before* their services were required. As a result, they were chosen to serve right in the very middle of the move of God, even though they weren't trained to operate in the role they found themselves in. What qualified them for the task at hand was not their training, nor their specific giftings. Rather, they were drafted into active service merely because they had come to the event already consecrated.

The principle contained in this story is truly amazing. At least it is to me. The ability to be used by God in a totally different way than the musicians had ever experienced took place simply because they showed up ready. The point, the focus, the intent of what I'm saying here is this: Consecration should be considered as a way of life for the followers of Christ. That is, if they want to be used of the Lord instead of merely hearing about some move of God, or perhaps even watching it unfold. To participate in what the Spirit is doing requires us to be ready before the "doing" ever begins.

That being the case, the first time act of consecration which takes place should not be considered as the only time such an action is necessary. As believers, we should make it a proactive goal to prayerfully set ourselves apart on a daily basis. In doing so, we will then be in a position to serve the will and way(s) of God as He sees fit, based on His timing, and intention. (See 1 Peter 2:9.)

Worship is obedient service manifesting through self-sacrifice.

COVENANT CONSIDERATIONS

One form of covenant is between two or more people in which there is a greater and a lesser. The greater oversees the lesser by agreeing to their request to enter into it. The lesser seeks to make covenant by submitting to the terms which the greater sets in place.

There are 4 basic components of a covenant:

1. Name
2. Place
3. Provision
4. Protection

One of the best Scriptural examples of covenant is found in the so-called "Lord's Prayer" (Mt. 6:9-13). However, it is not really His prayer as such. It's Jesus' instructive response to a request from His disciples as to how best they should pray. The prayer of Jesus (to the Father) is found in John 17.

Consider the words of Christ as He gave direction to the disciples:

> *"Our Father who is in heaven, Hallowed be Your name. Your kingdom come. Your will be done, on earth as it is in heaven. Give us this day our daily bread. And forgive us our debts, as we also have forgiven our debtors. And do not lead us into temptation,, but **deliver** us from evil. For Yours is the kingdom and the power and the glory forever. Amen."*
>
> (Emphasis added)

1. Name: The stronger gives their name (or shares their leadership covering) with the weaker in a commitment of integrity , faithfulness.
2. Place: The stronger grants the weaker rights and domain as if the land they own becomes legally shared with one another.
3. Protection: The stronger covers the weaker in regards to keeping them from harm (in any form it may come).
4. Provision: The resources of the stronger are equally shared with the weaker in order to sustain their life and the lives of those within their extended family, to the degree that is possible.

Most importantly, marriage is a *covenant* entered into by two people with an understanding that the vows they make to one another are taking place before God Almighty and are affirmed

by those gathered there with them. Making covenant is serious business. It is not something to be taken lightly. It is not done on a whim; it is not random; nor is it a passing or temporary thing. It requires heartfelt consideration, a humbled reverence, and honest intentions. When the words of a covenant are spoken they ascend up to God's throne where they are then sealed in heaven. That makes such an act profound indeed. *A covenant before God is meant to withstand any and all challenges that come against it.*

Jesus' Words Regarding Kingdom Covenant

The Kingdom Covenant is *the* context out of which every single aspect of one's spiritual faith walk is to flow. Its proclamation is the reason that Jesus came to earth (Lu. 4:4, 2 Cor. 5:18-21)

It is how Jesus identified the location of His kingdom (Jn. 18:36)

It is the topic which He told His disciples to focus on in their prayers (Mt. 6:10)

It is the #1 priority that He charged those who follow Him to make their own (Mt. 6:33)

It contains/embodies the principles, precepts, and protocol that God's people are to live by (Mt. 5:1-12, Mt. 5, 6, and 7).

As I see it, it is the most overlooked (and basically disregarded) topic in the global church today.

> *"Now having been questioned by the Pharisees as to when the kingdom of God was coming, He answered them and said, "The kingdom of God is not coming with signs to be observed; nor will they say, 'Look, here it is!' or, 'There it is!' For behold, the kingdom of God is in your midst."*
>
> ~Lu. 17:20, 21)

Jesus spoke those words to Pharisees, not to His followers as such. By doing so, He was fulfilling the objective which His Father had given Him—bringing the Kingdom in heaven down to earth. Even though the kingdom of God is eternal (with no beginning,

middle, or end), He nonetheless brought it directly to earth and introduced it into earth-time (or clock time), thereby making it possible for anyone and everyone who will accept it to enter not it. (See Acts 26:18, Col. 1:17.)

Corporate Covenants

Reading for context: Psalm 77:11-12

"Once again I'll go over what God has done, lay out on the table the ancient wonders; I'll ponder all the things you've accomplished, and give a long, loving look at your acts."

(MSG)

Text: Nehemiah 9

There are four basic components in a Corporate Covenant Contract. Each one is interconnected with the other and each one is essential to keeping it in place and active. They are:

1. Name (v.7)
2. Place (v.8)
3. Protection (vs.9-12)
4. Provision (v.15)

In order to activate a Corporate Covenant Contract, both parties are required to do three things:

1. Establish the terms of the Covenant (determine what it is to consist of)
2. Agree to the terms once they've been established (decide what it offers those seeking to have it put into effect)
3. Enter into the contract with a commitment to keeping it (declare that it has been accepted)

We must "enter in order to possess" (v.15c.)

A Peculiar People

Kingdom Citizenship Vs. Nationalized Christianity

Before I develop this narrative any further, I'll make four brief

statements. That way if you feel your blood pressure rising as you're reading them you can simply back away.

The Kingdom of God (Christ's kingdom) is not of this world. He said so Himself (Jn. 18:36). It is eternal, not temporal.

There are no national flags behind (or around) the throne of God (Deut. 5:7). NOTE: Most translations say "no other gods before Me." However the NASB says, "no other gods besides Me." I much prefer that concept. It seems considerably broader in what it encompasses.

The nation we were born into here on earth has absolutely nothing to do with the eternal citizenship of a follower of Christ (2 Peter 2:9). NOTE: Each component (category) of that passage is past tense, meaning that as followers of Christ, we are *already* included in each one. We don't have to earn them, grow into them, or perfect them. They came with our redemption package, so to speak.

> *"The government shall be upon HIS shoulders."*
> ~Isa. 9:6 (emphasis added)

I'll factor in the following definitions in order to help focus in on what I'm addressing:

KINGDOM (from the KJV Study Bible): n.

1. The territory or country subject to a king; an undivided territory under the dominion of a king or monarch.
2. The inhabitants or population subject to a king.
3. In natural history, a division; as the animal, vegetable and mineral kingdoms.
4. A region; a tract; the place where anything prevails and holds sway; as the watery kingdom.
5. In Scripture, the government or universal dominion of God. 1 Chron.29. Ps. 145.
6. The power of supreme administration. 1 Sam. 18.
7. A princely nation or state.
8. Heaven. Matt. 26.

9. State of glory in heaven. Matt. 5.

10. The reign of the Messiah. Matt. 3.

11. Government; rule; supreme administration.

KINGDOM (From Webster's): NOUN

a country, state, or territory ruled by a king or queen, i.e. "the Kingdom of the Netherlands"

synonyms:

realm · domain · dominion · country · land · nation · state · sovereign state

a realm associated with or regarded as being under the control of a particular person or thing, i.e. "the kingdom of dreams"

synonyms:

domain · province · realm · sphere · sphere/field of influence

the spiritual reign or authority of God.

the rule of God or Christ in a future age.

each of the three traditional divisions (animal, vegetable, and mineral) in which natural objects have conventionally been classified.

CITIZEN (from Scripture): n.

1. The native of a city, or an inhabitant who enjoys the freedom and privileges of the city in which he resides; the freeman of a city, as distinguished from a foreigner, or one not entitled to its franchises.

2. A townsman; a man of trade; not a gentleman.

3. An inhabitant; a dweller in any city, town or place.

4. In a general sense, a native or permanent resident in a city or country; as the citizens of London or Philadelphia; the citizens of the United States.

5. In the United States, a person, native or naturalized, who has the privilege of exercising the elective franchise, or the qualifications which enable him to vote for rulers, and to purchase and hold real estate.

CITIZENSHIP: adj. Having the qualities of a citizen.

(From Webster's) NOUN: The position or status of being a citizen of a particular country.

NATIONALISM (From Webster's): NOUN

Identification with one's own nation and support for its interests, especially to the exclusion or detriment of the interests of other nations. Advocacy of or support for the political independence of a particular nation or people.

CHRISTIANITY (from Scripture):

The name given by the Greeks or Romans, probably in reproach, to the followers of Jesus. It was first used at Antioch. The names by which the disciples were known among themselves were "brethren," "the faithful," "elect," "saints," "believers." But as distinguishing them from the multitude without, the name "Christian" came into use, and was universally accepted. This name occurs but three times in the New Testament (Acts 11:26; 26:28 ; 1 Peter 4:16)

(From Webster's)

The religion based on the person and teachings of Jesus of Nazareth, or its beliefs and practices. Christian quality or character.

POLITICS:

The activities associated with the government of a country or other area, especially the debate or conflict among individuals or parties having or hoping to achieve power. And, the activities of governments concerning the political relations between countries. And, the academic study of government and the stated activities within an organization that are aimed at improving someone's status or position and are typically considered to be devious or divisive.

A particular set of political beliefs or principles.

The assumptions or principles relating to or inherent in a sphere, theory, or thing, especially when concerned with power and status in a society.

I'll use but one verse to establish a foundation to build this narrative upon:

"The government shall be upon HIS shoulders."
~Isa. 9:6 (emphasis added)

How those who are not "born again" accept, relate, or conform to that verse is of little concern to me as I draft this out. My thoughts are directed solely to those who are followers of Christ, citizens of heaven, God's loyal and obedient subjects (His servants), His *worshipers. All those who are "in Christ Jesus" (Col. 3:1-3) have already been transferred into the Kingdom of God.

*Worship is obedient service manifesting through self-sacrifice.

> *"As you live this new life, we pray that you will be strengthened from God's boundless resources, so that you will find yourselves able to pass through any experience and endure it with courage. You will even be able to thank God in the midst of pain and distress because you are privileged to share the lot of those who are living in the light. For we must never forget that he rescued us from the power of darkness, and re-established us in the kingdom of his beloved Son, that is, in the kingdom of light. For it is by his Son alone that we have been redeemed and have had our sins forgiven."*
>
> ~Col. 1:13 (Phillips)

NOTE: This passage is past tense, as is 1 Peter 2:9. Meaning everything it states has already come to pass. It is therefore a proactive dynamic to be lived in and lived out of by "born again" believers.

Those of us who are branded/sealed (Eph. 4:30) as Christians have a personal and collective Scriptural charge (responsibility) to live our lives here on earth while at the same time functioning as citizens of an eternal Kingdom, which is not part of any earthly kingdom(s) as such.

Based on the level of sensitivity surrounding the subject of politics, I'd prefer not to deal with this topic at all. Just broaching it often leads to "fightin' words." Nonetheless, I have come to a place where I am convinced that the subject must be considered foundational as it relates to one's spiritual evolution and temporal

nationalistic citizenship. Here's why: Government has been an issue on earth ever since humankind walked out of "The Garden." You see, there is an aspect to living on the planet which we humans can't seem to get sorted out. It is this:

We resist (rebel against) having anyone or anything which attempt to have authority or take charge of our lives. The enemy of our souls had the exact same problem. *I'll address that later.*

We do that as individual persons as well as collectively as a people group (or nation). Without wandering out too far into such a theological minefield, I'll cautiously attempt to point out a pathway to walk from this side to the other, toward a safer (Biblically-based) place to stand regarding our political positioning, pundit posturing(s), and personal preferences.

Perhaps the best/simplest examples of Biblically historic power struggle is found in the story of the Tower of Babel.

"Now the whole earth used the same language and the same words. It came about as they journeyed east, that they found a plain in the land of Shinar and settled there. They said to one another, "Come, let us make bricks and burn them thoroughly." And they used brick for stone, and they used tar for mortar. They said, "Come, let us build for ourselves a city, and a tower whose top will reach into heaven, and let us make for ourselves a name, otherwise we will be scattered abroad over the face of the whole earth." The Lord came down to see the city and the tower which the sons of men had built. The Lord said, "Behold, they are one people, and they all have the same language. And this is what they began to do, and now nothing which they purpose to do will be impossible for them. Come, let Us go down and there confuse their language, so that they will not understand one another's speech." So the Lord scattered them abroad from there over the face of the whole earth; and they stopped building the city. Therefore its name was called Babel, because there the Lord confused the language of the whole earth; and from there the

Lord scattered them abroad over the face of the whole earth."
~Gen.11:1-9 (NASB)

That is a truly amazing story to ponder. To begin with, it is (or may be) the only place in Scripture where we find the three Persons of the Trinity conversing with themselves. The Lord makes an observational statement to the other two parties (v.6). Then He suggests to them that *they* should go down to earth and shake things up. The reason is clearly stated in v.6 which says, "This *is what they began to do, and now nothing which they purpose to do will be impossible for them."* In other words, the Creator Himself understands that the gift of creativity, which had been imparted directly into the DNA of humanity by His Divine hand (see Gen.1:1), when left unchecked—or ungoverned—can accomplish *anything!* That's what the text says.

The purposed intentions of the people in this story are twofold:
1. Let us make for ourselves a city *their* city
2. Let us make a name for ourselves

As I read this passage, I see the roots of two key negative/fallen human attributes manifesting. Firstly, a move toward self-aggrandizement (creating a self-centered-self-powered-self-driven-destiny). Secondly, a move toward self-governance—based on ego and personal achievement. If those things are key components in the political process, I don't know what is.

All strivings for power, control, fame, and recognition has at its base a political aspect. As such, moving in that direction and in those circles tends to separate those involved from this Scriptural truth:

All power and authority belong to God in Christ.

"Then Jesus came close to them and said, "All the authority of the universe has been given to me."'
~Mt. 28:18 (TPT)

My intention here isn't to challenge, correct, or condescend

toward anyone's personal political beliefs. Such matters are not
mine to involve myself with directly (see Ps. 131). How people
feel about politicians, party-lines, and government(s) in specific
isn't my concern. However, as a follower of Christ, it seems to me
that the political dynamics of kingdom citizenship should—at the
very least—be given some serious consideration as to what Jesus
said was to be the first priority of His followers (Mt. 6:33).

Seeking the Kingdom of God first and foremost is a charge
fashioned and framed around who (or what) is to be considered
as Sovereign in the lives of Christians. I am merely attempting
to convey what I understand to be a Biblically-based perspective
regarding how believers are to view temporal government(s), politics,
and politicians. This is meant to draw a comparison between how
such things are to be evaluated and addressed from two separate
viewpoints. One is temporal, earth-based, and established within
the framework of earth-time. The other is eternal, formed outside
of time (with no beginning, middle, or end). One is man-made, and
limited to usage here on this planet. The other is God-designed,
without limits, and intended to function throughout eternity. One
changes based on shifts in culture, historical transitions, and the
process of life and death. The other never changes—having only One
Sovereign Ruler over the subjects/citizens of a heavenly Kingdom.
Scripturally speaking, that's known as the Kingdom of God.

Here's another story from Biblical history that presents a picture
of how spiritual life is impacted by politics:

> "...While Joshua was there near Jericho: He looked up and
> saw right in front of him a man standing, holding his drawn
> sword. Joshua stepped up to him and said, "Whose side are you
> on—ours or our enemies'?" He said, "Neither. I'm commander
> of God's army."
>
> ~Jos. 5:13, 14 (MSG)

If you were to hold that verse up and let light refract through it,

you might see an aspect of the politics of opposing sides reflected in the interchange. Joshua is concerned about taking sides—an earthbound perspective. He is, after all, earthbound in his concerns. While at the same time, the angel is not from around here. He was sent from eternity, representing God's government and God's way of discharging His Divine authority. So, his response is neither on behalf of one side, nor the other. His statement validates the positional directive which came from the throne of God—the seat of eternal governance.

To repeat: I'm not taking sides or trying to build a case (pro or con) for the political processes of earthly government(s). That's not anywhere near my intention. I'm trying to clarify/inform/remind anyone who's reading this that the *whos* and *hows* of any and all forms of earth-based government(s) have no lasting/eternal value in terms of the kingdom of God and those who occupy it. When any form of man-made/man-led government is allowed to become so inner-linked into how the governance of Jehovah is designed to function, there is a grave danger of the temporal forms supplanting the eternal one.

I'm attempting to make a comparison between "Kingdom Citizenship" and "Nationalized Christianity" in order to point out the distinctions which should exist—but increasingly don't. At least not as I see such distinctions in these daze we're living in.

Another example from Scripture…

This happened when the political leader of the day (Herod) took steps to remove his competition:

Now after Jesus was born in Bethlehem of Judea in the days of Herod the king, behold, wise men from the east came to Jerusalem, saying, "Where is he who has been born king of the Jews? For we saw his star when it rose and have come to worship him." When Herod the king heard this, he was troubled, and all Jerusalem with him; and assembling all the chief priests and scribes of the people, he inquired of them where the Christ was to be born. They told him, "In Bethlehem of Judea, for so it is

written by the prophet: "And you, O Bethlehem, in the land of Judah, are by no means least among the rulers of Judah; for from you **shall come a ruler** *who will shepherd my people Israel.'"...* **Herod is about to search for the child, to destroy him."**
~Mt. 2 (emphasis added)

As was then, so is now—politics can get very ugly indeed.

Out of many more Scriptural narratives, there are a few more worth pondering:

The most dangerous counter-cultural-terrorist in opposition to the kingdom of God is satan. His pit-fall (pun intended) was based solely on his prideful desire for political dominance. He had power and control issues. His intent was to rule the universe. Pride was at the very heart of his downfall.

> *"Lift yourself up with pride and you will soon be brought low..."*
> ~Pro. 29:23a (TPT)

> *"But you said in your heart, 'I will ascend to heaven; I will raise my throne above the stars of God, and I will sit on the mount of assembly in the recesses of the north. I will ascend above the heights of the clouds; I will make myself like the Most High.'"*
> ~Isa. 14:13, 14 (NASB)

Consider 1 Peter 5:6 which provides us a clear and concise explanation of how pride can lead to all sorts of chaos, personal and corporate drama, and a totally misdirected comprehension of what it means to serve in obedience, yielded to a Sovereign King as a loyal citizen in His kingdom.

> *"If you bow low in God's awesome presence, he will eventually exalt you as you leave the timing in his hands."*
> ~1 Peter 5:6 (TPT)

It's our job to humble ourselves. It's God's job to exalt us (on His terms , in His timing). If we insist on doing His job, He has no choice but to do ours.

God's either in charge or He's not. He's either Sovereign or He's not. He's either the One True God over all His creation or He's not. The government is either on His shoulders or it's not. See a pattern here?

THE BROKEN ONES
(Ps. 51:17)

When you bow down, way down
You may find a place where few have gone
And if you stay down, stay way down
You may see some things that few are shown

If you'll humble yourself under His mighty hand
He will lift you up, and steady you to stand

He will embrace the broken ones…

When you give up, really give up
You can find your place of sweet release
And if you'll give up, completely give up
God will flood your heart with perfect peace

If you'll humble yourself under His mighty hand
He will lift you up, and steady you to stand

He will embrace the broken ones…

~W. Berry / See & Say Songs, BMI

I'm not meaning to mess with anyone's political preferences as such, nor their voting history. How one's affiliations and loyalties are established concerning their homeland is, for the most part, none of my business or my concern. However, here in America, how one sorts through subjects like *patriotism, national pride, and service-to-country is between them and their own conscience I suppose. (See Heb. 11:14.)

I personally don't see a way for followers of Christ to reconcile the elevation of nationalistic pride (mind-set or heart-set) above that of their Kingdom birthright without creating theological inconsistency, corporate disunity, unclarified testimony, and a general weakening of Biblically-based principles, precepts, and core values. I am aware that may just be me stating my personal point of view. That being said, this is, after all, a book based on my own pondering(s) of things such as this. So, there ya go.

*Patriotism or national pride is the feeling of love, devotion and sense of attachment to a homeland and alliance with other citizens who share the same sentiment. This attachment can be a combination of many different feelings relating to one's own homeland, including ethnic, cultural, political or historical aspects. It encompasses a set of concepts closely related to nationalism. (Wikipedia)

A disclaimer (of a sort): My concern isn't in regards to the structure of temporal government(s) or the process of politics as such. I am well aware of what Scriptures has to say about temporal leadership and the structures they operate from.

> Be a good citizen. All governments are under God. Insofar as there is peace and order, it's God's order. So live responsibly as a citizen. If you're irresponsible to the state, then you're irresponsible with God, and God will hold you responsible. Duly constituted authorities are only a threat if you're trying to get by with something. Decent citizens should have nothing to fear. Do you want to be on good terms with the government? Be a responsible citizen and you'll get on just fine, the government

working to your advantage. But if you're breaking the rules right and left, watch out. The police aren't there just to be admired in their uniforms. God also has an interest in keeping order, and he uses them to do it. That's why you must live responsibly—not just to avoid punishment but also because it's the right way to live.

~Rom. 13:1-5 (MSG)

"Remind people to respect their governmental leaders on every level as law-abiding citizens and to be ready to fulfill their civic duty. And remind them to never tear down anyone with their words or quarrel, but instead be considerate, humble, and courteous to everyone."

~Titus 3:1, 2 (TPT)

In order to honor the Lord, you must respect and defer to the authority of every human institution, whether it be the highest ruler or the governors he puts in place to punish lawbreakers and to praise those who do what's right. For it is God's will for you to silence the ignorance of foolish people by doing what is right. As God's loving servants, you should live in complete freedom, but never use your freedom as a cover-up for evil. Recognize the value of every person and continually show love to every believer. Live your lives with great reverence and in holy awe of God. Honor your rulers. Those who are servants, submit to the authority of those who are your masters—not only to those who are kind and gentle but even to those who are hard and difficult. You find God's favor by deciding to please God even when you endure hardships because of unjust suffering. For what merit is it to endure mistreatment for wrongdoing? Yet if you are mistreated when you do what is right, and you faithfully endure it, this is commendable before God. In fact, you were called to live this way, because Christ also suffered in your place, leaving you his example for you to follow. He never sinned and he never spoke deceitfully. When he was verbally abused, he

did not return with an insult; when he suffered, he would not threaten retaliation. Jesus faithfully entrusted himself into the hands of God, who judges righteously. He himself carried our sins in his body on the cross so that we would be dead to sin and live for righteousness. Our instant healing flowed from his wounding. You were like sheep that continually wandered away but now you have returned to the true Shepherd of your lives—the kind Guardian who lovingly watches over your souls.

~1 Peter 2:13-25 (TPT)

My real concern, the one that's currently breaking my heart, is that so many followers of Christ are living at variance with one another based on how they are misunderstanding temporal-earth-bound-governance and the politics which flows from it. It is sad, so sad, to know that believers who will live together eternally in the glorious afterlife—with the Father, Son, Holy Ghost, and a myriad of all those who have been "accepted into the beloved" (Eph. 1:6)—can't find unity amid diversity here on earth in such matters. As Christians, the so-called left and right should be finding Biblically-appropriate ways of coming to terms with exactly whose government they are submitted to and living under.

Yes, we are called to yield to and obey the laws of the land we're in. But, there is a high level of submission and service to which God's Word calls us. When we allow any person, place, or thing to override the command given in Deuteronomy 5:7, the results are tragic on a personal as well as a collective/corporate level.

"You shall have no other gods before Me."

~Deut. 5:7 (NASB)

Footnotes:

*Deuteronomy 5:7

The politics of the Kingdom of God is the system His people are to represent here on earth as it is in heaven (Mt. 6:10). Those who have been transferred from darkness into light (Col. 1:13) are to live in and out of 1 Peter 2:9. Otherwise, our ability to carry out the

"ministry of reconciliation" (our job description) as "ambassadors for Christ" (our job title) simply isn't possible to fulfill with any degree of honesty, integrity, and authenticity.

> *All this is from God, who through Christ reconciled us to himself and gave us the ministry of reconciliation; that is, in Christ God was reconciling the world to himself, not counting their trespasses against them, and entrusting to us the message of reconciliation. Therefore, we are ambassadors for Christ, God making his appeal through us. We implore you on behalf of Christ, be reconciled to God. For our sake he made him to be sin who knew no sin, so that in him we might become the righteousness of God.*
>
> ~2 Cor. 5:18-21

The reason we're saved isn't to get to heaven. That's a by-product of redemption. If that were the case, once we received salvation, we'd have gone directly to heaven. Since we're still here on earth, there must be a reason. There is. It's presented clearly and distinctly in 2 Corinthians 5. Putting what it says we are to do into daily, ongoing practice is why I'm writing this.

In closing, think this through:

> *"Don't hoard treasure down here where it gets eaten by moths and corroded by rust or—worse!—stolen by burglars. Stockpile treasure in heaven, where it's safe from moth and rust and burglars. It's obvious, isn't it? The place where your treasure is, is the place you will most want to be, and end up being."*
>
> ~Mt. 6:21 (MSG)

> *"Thy kingdom come, Thy will be done, on earth as it is in heaven."*
>
> ~Mt. 6:10

64

Here's a somewhat lighter POV....

GLENDALE, CA—A man was rushed to the hospital yesterday after encountering a slightly different viewpoint than his own.

Shortly before 12:30 p.m., Glendale PD officers responded to a 911 call at the Java Lounge Coffee House in the 900 block of North Emerson Road. They found a person who had collapsed in shock and went to the station for help. Witnesses say the man was having a casual conversation about politics with another patron when the minutely opposing viewpoint was expressed.

"They were both Democrats, Bernie supporters," said Janice Hughson, a barista at the Java Lounge. "Then the guy he was talking to said he had some issues with abortion and thinks there should at least be a few limitations put on the practice. That's when the man seized up and began foaming at the mouth. It was terrible."

Four other bystanders were also emotionally injured by the moderately divergent opinion but were not hospitalized.

The man is being kept stable on ideology support at St. Francis medical center, surrounded by friends and family who agree with him 100% on every single issue.

The man who suggested the slightly differing opinion fled the scene.

Anyone with information is asked to alert the authorities.

(From: babylonbee.com)

"Battle lines being drawn, nobody's right, if everybody's wrong..."

~S. Stills

Two resources for consideration:
The Most Important Person On Earth by Myles Munroe
The Way of the Dragon or the Way of the Lamb: Searching for Jesus' Part of Power in a Church that Has Abandoned It by Jamin Goggin and Kyle Strobel

The Rx For Curing Nationalized Religion(s)

> *"Of the increase of his government and of peace there shall be no end, on the throne of David, and on his kingdom, to establish it, and to uphold it with justice and with righteousness from that time on, even forever. The zeal of the Lord of hosts will perform this."*
> ~Isa. 9:7 (NHE)

Considering that the kingdom of God is eternal (and it is), with no beginning middle, or end, then perhaps we should each ask ourselves the following question:

If the country which we consider as our homeland were to no longer exist, would God's kingdom still be active, accessible, and expanding?

An inner-related thought is that *Christianity* and *Capitalism* are not synonyms. Neither are *Patriotism* and *Nationalism*.

Selah (pause , ponder)

Transcending Tribalism
TRIBALISM: NOUN

The state or fact of being organized in a tribe or tribes. The behavior and attitudes that stem from strong loyalty to one's own tribe or social group. (Webster's)

Humanity is being fractured on a global level by tribalism. Families, communities, regions, and nations are facing off at one another with a variance and divisiveness which makes the concept of unity virtually impossible. The depth and breadth of that reality goes far beyond my ability to effectively address it by offering a fix for humankind's disjointed condition. I can however present a model for those who consider themselves to be Christian in their beliefs and how they're lived out. It's found in Scripture.

> *"And God has made all things new, and reconciled us to himself, and given us the ministry of reconciling others to God.*

In other words, it was through the Anointed One that God was shepherding the world, not even keeping records of their transgressions, and **he has entrusted to us the ministry of opening the door of reconciliation to God. We are ambassadors of the Anointed One who carry the message of Christ to the world,** *as though God were tenderly pleading with them directly through our liPs. So we tenderly plead with you on Christ's behalf, "Turn back to God and be reconciled to him." For God made the only one who did not know sin to become sin for us, so that we who did not know righteousness might become the righteousness of God through our union with him."*

~2 Cor. 5:18-21 (TPT)

Followers of Christ can only hope to carry out such a Biblically-based charge by purposing to first accept what that text is saying, and then commit to becoming proactive by implementing it in real time and in real life—through the presence, power, and purpose of the Holy Spirit. I see no other way for unity to begin taking shape, without God's people moving together, linked into such a mandate.

"How truly wonderful and delightful to see brothers and sisters living together in sweet unity! It's as precious as the sacred scented oil flowing from the head of the high priest Aaron, dripping down upon his beard and running all the way down to the hem of his priestly robes. This heavenly harmony can be compared to the dew dripping down from the skies upon Mount Hermon, refreshing the mountain slopes of Israel. For from this realm of sweet harmony God will release his eternal blessing, the promise of life forever!"

~Ps. 133 (TPT)

There's another passage which speaks directly to how an individual can begin putting the "ministry of reconciliation" and their "ambassadorship for Christ" together.

"With what shall I come before the Lord, and bow myself before God on high? Shall I come before him with burnt offerings, with calves a year old? Will the Lord be pleased with thousands of rams, with ten thousands of rivers of oil? Shall I give my firstborn for my transgression, the fruit of my body for the sin of my soul?" He has told you, O man, what is good; and what does the Lord require of you but to do justice, and to love kindness, and to walk humbly with your God?"

~Micah 6:6-8

I'll include an alternate rendering because I like the picture it presents.

"How can I stand up before God and show proper respect to the high God? Should I bring an armload of offerings topped off with yearling calves? Would God be impressed with thousands of rams, with buckets and barrels of olive oil? Would he be moved if I sacrificed my firstborn child, my precious baby, to cancel my sin? But he's already made it plain how to live, what to do, what God is looking for in men and women. It's quite simple: Do what is fair and just to your neighbor, be compassionate and loyal in your love, and don't take yourself too seriously—take God seriously."

~Micah 6:6-8 (MSG)

The directive in that passage points to three things in specific which are required (on a personal level) in order to position oneself as a unifier rather than a divider. Keep in mind that the process of implementing reconciliation is not to birth some sort of grand movement. Such a reformation must be approached on a person-to-person basis. If a wide-reaching movement is to take shape, it can only happen as individuals begin to apply the principles and precepts of what is encouraged by the included Scriptural passages.

- Do justice: To do justice is to learn it, embrace it, and then live it out in daily life.

- Love kindness: To love kindness is to respond to it emotionally, mentally, and spiritually. It is in essence participation in the so called "Golden Rule."

"Here is a simple, rule-of-thumb guide for behavior: Ask yourself what you want people to do for you, then grab the initiative and do it for them. Add up God's Law and Prophets and this is what you get."

~Matt. 7:12-14 (MSG)

- Walk humbly: To walk humbly with your God is first and foremost a sign of yielded obedience to the Sovereign that you serve. For Christians exactly who that is can be answered simply with only one verse from the Bible.

"Thou shall have no other gods besides me"

~Deut. 5:7 (NASB)

My intention here isn't to debate, dissuade, criticize, or condemn other forms or aspects of religion. I am personally a follower of Christ, a "born again" believer, and a citizen of God's eternal Kingdom (1 Peter 2:9). I serve the King of kings, Christ Jesus, the Lord of lords. My position in regards to what I'm stating in this narrative—and throughout this entire book—is this:

"...Fear God. Worship him in total commitment. Get rid of the gods your ancestors worshiped on the far side of The River (the Euphrates) and in Egypt. You, worship God. If you decide that it's a bad thing to worship God, then choose a god you'd rather serve—and do it today. Choose one of the gods your ancestors worshiped from the country beyond The River, or one of the gods of the Amorites, on whose land you're now living. As for me and my family, we'll worship God."

~Joshua 24:14, 15 (MSG)

UNITY
(Ps. 133)

Behold how good and pleasant it is
When believers are gathered in unity
It's like the dew of Hermon
Coming down on Mt. Zion
Where the people of God see their destiny

There the Lord commands a blessing
When He hears us all rejoicing
In the bound that's been created
Through the blood of our Redeemer

CHORUS:
He gives us life forevermore
Life forevermore
Life forevermore
When we are united in Him

Behold how good and pleasant it is
To be seated with God in the heavenlies
It like the dew of Hermon
Coming down on Mt. Zion
And washing away our iniquity

REPEAT CHORUS:

~W. Berry / See & Say Songs, BMI

The Path(s) Of The Righteous:
Spring(s), Highway(s), Wells(s), and Room(s)

There is only one entranceway into the Kingdom, in and through Christ Jesus (Jn. 14:6). However, there are numerous ways of arriving at the gateway.

> *"Blessed are those whose strength is in you, in whose heart are the highways to Zion."*
>
> ~Ps. 84:5

> *"With joy you will draw water from the wells of salvation."*
>
> ~Isa. 12:3

> *"...all my springs are in you."*
>
> ~Ps. 87:7b

> *"In my Father's house are many rooms."*
>
> ~Jn. 14:2

The plural designation(s) mentioned in each of those verses can far too often be overlooked. When that takes place, the way(s) to reach God—and be sustained by His provision—can be perceived as considerably more limited than Scripture states they are. That is to say, God's mercy and grace (Heb. 4:16) provide multiple pathways and abundant sources of provision to enable the quest for the Kingdom to be successfully navigated. The perspective I'm stating is one of personal theology. You may (or may not) agree with my point of view regarding dynamic pathways(s). Nonetheless, the wording from Scripture there being more than one way to arrive at the desired destination is in fact Biblically based.

To better clarify what I'm addressing, consider the following lyrics. They are from the very first song I composed after returning back to a restored position *in the house* having spent 15 years or so as a prodigal.

CHILDREN OF LIGHT
(Eph. 5:8)

Some turn to God in their childhood
Some turn to God in the street
Some turn to God in their sorrow
But, thank God, there's still room at his feet

I was lost like a ship on the wild sea
Tossed on the high tide of sin
I was goin' down for the last time
But, God threw out his lifeline
And, He lead me to the harbor again

CHORUS #1:
We are the children of light
The road up ahead stays bright
God calls us to follow, the straight and the narrow
And, He shines like a beacon in the night
We are the children of light

Every man has a burden to carry
Every woman has pain that don't show
But every child of the faith has their own hiding place
Where the caries of this world just can't go

CHORUS #2:
We are the children of light
The road up ahead stays bright
God calls us to follow the straight and the narrow
And, He shines through His son so bright
We are His children of light

~W. Berry / See & Say Songs, BMI

From one's youth, from the street(s), or from personal sorrow(s). Weighted down from burden bearing, or processing pain. Each of those conditions, along with seemingly countless other human frailties, can serve as the driving source of seeking deliverance, freedom, and ultimately salvation.

There is only one way into the Kingdom of God. But, there are many pathways that lead to the entrance in (and through) Christ Jesus. *"Let all the thirsty come"* is a call to anyone and everyone. Where they are called from will differ. The course(s) taken will also be varied. But, through conviction, confession, repentance, and conversion (redemption), the entrance comes down to seeking , finding. And, that is what the charge of Mt. 6:33 will always be based upon. That's the very essence of questing for the Kingdom.

> *God has made everything beautiful in its time. Also, he has put eternity into man's heart, yet so that he cannot find out what God has done from the beginning to the end.*
>
> ~Ecc. 3:11b

WAYS OF SEEING , BEING INSIDE
Who's In Charge? / Staying with the Baggage / Payment in Full

Biblically speaking, there are numerous guidelines for how to see and be involved with/in Kingdom life. I'll close our this chapter by briefly mentioning just three examples to ponder:

Who's In Charge Of The Kingdom?

> *Woe to him who strives with him who formed him, a pot among earthen pots! Does the clay say to him who forms it, 'What are you making?' or 'Your work has no handles'? Woe to him who says to a father, 'What are you begetting?' or to a woman, 'With what are you in labor?' Thus says the Lord the Holy One of Israel, and the one who formed him: 'Ask me of things to come;*

will you command me concerning my children and the work of my hands? I made the earth and created man on it....'"

~Isa. 45:9-12

(Also see Job 38-42 / Isa. 40:12-31 / Rom. 9:21)

How's is equity achieved in the kingdom?

"Now when David and his men came to Ziklag on the third day, the Amalekites had made a raid against the Negeb and against Ziklag. They had overcome Ziklag and burned it with fire and taken captive the women and all who were in it, both small and great. They killed no one, but carried them off and went their way. And when David and his men came to the city, they found it burned with fire, and their wives and sons and daughters taken captive. Then David and the people who were with him raised their voices and wept until they had no more strength to weep. David's two wives also had been taken captive, Ahinoam of Jezreel and Abigail the widow of Nabal of Carmel. And David was greatly distressed, for the people spoke of stoning him, because all the people were bitter in soul, each for his sons and daughters. But David strengthened himself in the Lord his God. And David said to Abiathar the priest, the son of Ahimelech, "Bring me the ephod." So Abiathar brought the ephod to David. And David inquired of the Lord, "Shall I pursue after this band? Shall I overtake them?" He answered him, "Pursue, for you shall surely overtake and shall surely rescue." So David set out, and the six hundred men who were with him, and they came to the brook Besor, where those who were left behind stayed. But David pursued, he and four hundred men. Two hundred stayed behind, who were too exhausted to cross the brook Besor. They found an Egyptian in the open country and brought him to David. And they gave him bread and he ate. They gave him water to drink, and they gave him a piece of a cake of figs and two clusters of raisins. And when he had

eaten, his spirit revived, for he had not eaten bread or drunk water for three days and three nights. And David said to him, "To whom do you belong? And where are you from?" He said, "I am a young man of Egypt, servant to an Amalekite, and my master left me behind because I fell sick three days ago. We had made a raid against the Negeb of the Cherethites and against that which belongs to Judah and against the Negeb of Caleb, and we burned Ziklag with fire." And David said to him, "Will you take me down to this band?" And he said, "Swear to me by God that you will not kill me or deliver me into the hands of my master, and I will take you down to this band." And when he had taken him down, behold, they were spread abroad over all the land, eating and drinking and dancing, because of all the great spoil they had taken from the land of the Philistines and from the land of Judah. And David struck them down from twilight until the evening of the next day, and not a man of them escaped, except four hundred young men, who mounted camels and fled. David recovered all that the Amalekites had taken, and David rescued his two wives. Nothing was missing, whether small or great, sons or daughters, spoil or anything that had been taken. David brought back all. David also captured all the flocks and herds, and the people drove the livestock before him, and said, "This is David's spoil." Then David came to the two hundred men who had been too exhausted to follow David, and who had been left at the brook Besor. And they went out to meet David and to meet the people who were with him. And when David came near to the people he greeted them. Then all the wicked and worthless fellows among the men who had gone with David said, "Because they did not go with us, we will not give them any of the spoil that we have recovered, except that each man may lead away his wife and children, and depart." But David said, "You shall not do so, my brothers, with what the Lord has given us. He has preserved us and given into our hand the band that came against us. Who would listen to you

in this matter? **For as his share is who goes down into the battle, so shall his share be who stays by the baggage.** *They shall share alike." And he made it a statute and a rule for Israel from that day forward to this day.*

~1 Sam. 30:1-2

What's The Pay Rate For Service In The Kingdom?

*"For the kingdom of heaven is like a master of a house who went out early in the morning to hire laborers for his vineyard. After agreeing with the laborers for a denarius a day, he sent them into his vineyard. And going out about the third hour he saw others standing idle in the marketplace, and to them he said, 'You go into the vineyard too, and whatever is right I will give you.' So they went. Going out again about the sixth hour and the ninth hour, he did the same. And about the eleventh hour he went out and found others standing. And he said to them, 'Why do you stand here idle all day?' They said to him, 'Because no one has hired us.' He said to them, 'You go into the vineyard too.' And when evening came, the owner of the vineyard said to his foreman, 'Call the laborers and pay them their wages, beginning with the last, up to the first.' And when those hired about the eleventh hour came, each of them received a denarius. Now when those hired first came, they thought they would receive more, but each of them also received a denarius. And on receiving it they grumbled at the master of the house, saying, 'These last worked only one hour, and you have made them equal to us who have borne the burden of the day and the scorching heat.' But he replied to one of them, 'Friend, I am doing you no wrong. Did you not agree with me for a denarius? Take what belongs to you and go. **I choose to give to this last worker as I give to you. Am I not allowed to do what I choose with what belongs to me?** Or do you begrudge my generosity? So the last will be first, and the first last."*

~Mt. 20:1-16 (emphasis added)

All three of these passages are dealing with Sovereignty—who's in charge and who's not. The foundational (or grounding) Old Testament text that addresses this is Deuteronomy 5:7, which has to do with consecration, covenant and worship on a basic Biblical level. The New Testament passage linked to that commandment principle is found in Romans 12:1, 2 (see MSG.)

Worship is obedient service manifesting through self-sacrifice. (Wayne-Speak)

Everything I've mentioned above has to do with how followers of Christ understand and respond to what Jesus said is to be the #1 response-ability of each and every believer:

"Seek first the kingdom of God and His righteousness..."
~Mt. 6:33

Section Three
THE COMMITMENT

AN UPSIDE-DOWN KINGDOM (IN A WACKED-OUT WORLD)

While working on this manuscript, I am also reading a new book by Timothy Keller entitled, *Hope In Times Of Fear*. In it, he presents a very clear and concise narrative regarding the two ways of seeing (perceiving/approaching) God's kingdom—embodied in and expressed through the life of Jesus Christ.

> "The world's expectation was for a Messiah to come once. Instead Jesus announces a Messiah who comes twice, and that means something completely unlooked for—a Messiah who comes twice comes the first time in weakness, not strength. That is why the two-stage kingdom is, from the world's point of view, the "upside-down" kingdom. This King comes in a way that reverses the values of the world. He comes in weakness and service, not strength and force, to die as a ransom for us.
>
> There is *retributive reversal*, in which the desired successes of sinful living end up being curses. The freedom and reward sin appears to offer become slavery and curse. Sin has

a boomerang effect, so that those who betray will be betrayed, those who lie will be lied to, those who live by the sword will die by the sword. Second, there is *redemptive reversal,* in which God chooses the weak over the powerful, the foolish over the wise, in order to save the world. And then God saves *through* the weakness, not despite it.

The remarkable message of the Bible, then, is: "Everyone is ultimately caught in the matrix of one of these two…patterns of living." (Gregory K. Beale). The good things of the world seen as blessings (beauty, power, comfort, success, recognition) but received without God become curses. They will drive you and consume you. And so the most just thing God can do to those who reject him is to give them up to what they want (Rom. 1:21-23). However, the hard things of this world seen as curses (weakness, deprivation, loss and rejection) but received with faith in God will be turned into blessings (2 Cor. 4:16, 17). Every person lives within one of these matrices; each one of us is traveling along one trajectory or the other.

The kind of commitment being addressed here isn't the one we make at the point of our conversion. Adherence to the principles, precepts, and practices presented in Scripture—after redemption occurs—has to do with follow through, not the act of receiving salvation. Personal experience with redemption most certainly has a heartfelt surrender in it. But, the depth of that encounter should change (deepen) over time as our relationship to (and with) the Father, Son, and Holy Kingdom evolves. It should mature as we "grow up" in matters related to life in and of the Kingdom. (See Eph. 4:11-16 , Col. 1:9-12).

Consider the following text:

> "So **if** you're serious about living this new resurrection life with Christ, act like it. Pursue the things over which Christ presides. Don't shuffle along, eyes to the ground, absorbed with the things

right in front of you. Look up, and be alert to what is going on around Christ—that's where the action is. See things from his perspective. Your old life is dead. Your new life, which is your real life—even though invisible to spectators—is with Christ in God. He is your life. When Christ (your real life, remember) shows up again on this earth, you'll show up, too—the real you, the glorious you. Meanwhile, be content with obscurity, like Christ."

~Col. 3:1-4 (MSG) emphasis added

In this passage, Paul is addressing believers. His comments aren't directed toward any other grouping of people. Notice the word *if* in the text. It is a qualifier that implies there is an option to pursue—a quest to take up. It is being mentioned for those who are already in the faith, so to speak. The intent of the text is that those who are earnest about their commitment should learn to focus their thoughts on things above, instead of things on earth. (See Rom. 12:1, 2 / MSG)

The KJV uses the word *affection* regarding such a pursuit. The ESV renders it as *mind*. In Greek, *affection* means to exercise the mind; to be disposed in a certain mental direction; to interest oneself in (with concern or obedience). It comes from a root word meaning *development of cognitive faculties* or *understanding*. That is to say, how one thinks about matters related to an eternal relationship with Kingdom issues.

The passage isn't dealing with the personal security of one's salvation. That's not the point of the text. The focus is on establishing a priority for living out a redeemed life here in real time in the real world. If you'll fine tune your focus, you may begin to see Matthew 6:33 being outworked in Paul's narrative.

"If ye then be risen with Christ, seek those things which are above, where Christ sitteth on the right hand of God. Set your affection on things above, not on things on the earth. For ye are

dead, and your life is hid with Christ in God. When Christ, who is our life, shall appear, then shall ye also appear with him in glory."

~Col. 3:1-4 (KJV) emphasis added)

Paul isn't dealing with the matter of eternal security as such, since he's writing to those who are "in the house" already. Rather, he's saying that there is a way of living out one's faith that calls us out (beyond/above) our redemption. That is the essence of the quest, the basis for Kingdom seeking.

Look again at how MSG renders the last phrase in the text under consideration. It says, "be content with obscurity, like Christ." That relates directly to the directive in Philippians 2:5-8.

> *"Have this mind among yourselves, which is yours in Christ Jesus, who, though he was in the form of God, did not count equality with God a thing to be grasped, but emptied himself, by taking the form of a servant, being born in the likeness of men. And being found in human form, he humbled himself by becoming obedient to the point of death, even death on a cross."*

Notice the use of the word *mind* in that passage. It is the same Greek word that is used in the Colossians 3 passage. Clearly, the aspect of mental ascension is an essential component of a committed and proactive lifestyle of belief. Or, it should be.

> *"For as he thinks in his heart, so is he."*

~Pro. 23:7a

The same perspective can be seen in Romans 12:2:

> *"Do not be conformed to this world, but be transformed by the renewal of your mind, that by testing you may discern what is the will of God, what is good and acceptable and perfect."*

Once again, *mind* is the same word used in both the Philippians 2 and the Colossians 3 passages. Our mental comprehension and appreciation are presented and defined in a way that should not be diminished.

The level of human IQ is not a singular point for consideration in matters related to a Kingdom commitment. However, mental adherence should not be relegated to a lower level of importance in such matters.

Scripture tells us there are four distinct areas of commitment that are of equal importance in regards to how we live out a lifestyle that reflects who we are in Christ. They are distinct, but not separate. Together they make up a collective whole—a complete person.

ALL IN: HEART, SOUL, STRENGTH, AND MIND

> *"You shall love the Lord your God with all your heart, and with all your soul and with all your strength, and with all your mind."*
>
> ~Lu. 10:27

A total commitment calls for a total surrender. As I've mentioned in previous chapters already…worship is obedient service manifesting through self-sacrifice. (Wayne-Speak)

The verse above breaks down a total commitment to God into four specific areas. Therefore, from a mathematic perspective, a 100% commitment would be based on four sections of 25% each:

Heart = 25%, Soul = 25%, Strength = 25%, Mind = 25%, for a total of 100%. All four components are of equal value. None is more important than the other. Consider the meaning of each aspect based on their Greek definitions:

- Heart—Thoughts, feelings, emotions
- Soul—Breath, spirit, human essence
- Strength—Forcefulness, power
- Mind—Thinking, disposition, imagination, understanding

"Belief is not merely intellectual assent but it is heart faith that brings salvation…it is more than looking at the evidence and working it all out, but is not less than that. Faith includes the mind—how else will it be an act of the entire person?"

~Timothy Keller

Let me be clear about what I'm saying. My comments have nothing to do with salvation as such. I am addressing the nature of a commitment to the Kingdom *after* redemption has occurred. The key word to be considered in the Luke 10:27 text is the word *all*. It's stated four times, coming just before the words *heart, soul, strength,* and *mind.* Therefore, the commandment is saying that a total commitment to loving the Lord God has to do with a 100%, full-on expression of that love in each of the four areas mentioned. That is to say, a life given to God is to be measured by the level shown in all four categories combined. Rendered that way, the directive of having a singular God to worship and serve becomes much clearer.

Such a commitment can be understood as grounded on Deuteronomy 5:7, which states, *"Thou shall have no other gods before Me."* (KJV) The NASB uses the word *besides* instead of *before.*

THE SHEMA: AN OVERVIEW

Historically, the understanding of how such a commitment is to be manifested is rooted in the Old Testament, expressed in the Jewish faith through the Shema.

"Hear, O Israel: The Lord our God, the Lord is one. You shall love the Lord your God with all your heart and with all your soul and with all your might. And these words that I command you today shall be on your heart. You shall teach them diligently to your children, and shall talk of them when you sit in your house, and when you walk by the way, and when you lie down, and when you rise.

~Deut. 6:4-7

In the Jewish faith tradition, the Deuteronomy 6 text mentioned above is known as the Shema.

> "The Shema is the title of a prayer that Jews recite twice daily, every morning and every evening. This prayer, often considered the most important prayer in Judaism, is taken from Scripture and is composed of Deuteronomy 6:4–9, Deuteronomy 11:13–21, and Numbers 15:37–41. These recitations of Scripture are meant to express a commitment of loyalty to keeping covenant with God by loving Him fully, obeying His ways, and teaching children to do the same.
>
> The prayer is called the Shema because *Shema* is the first word of the prayer in Hebrew.
>
> In Hebrew, *shema* does not simply mean "hear" as in ears perceiving sound and the brain processing information. Rather *shema* means listening, taking heed, and responding with action to what has been heard. So this twice daily prayer calls Jews to live out their commitment to God, putting into practice their love for Him.
>
> Jesus references the Shema in Mark 12:28–31 when responding to the question of which commandment is the most important. "And one of the scribes came up and heard them disputing with one another, and seeing that he answered them well, asked him, 'Which commandment is the most important of all?' Jesus answered, 'The most important is, "Hear, O Israel: The Lord our God, the Lord is one. And you shall love the Lord your God with all your heart and with all your soul and with all your mind and with all your strength." The second is this: "You shall love your neighbor as yourself." There is no other commandment greater than these.'" Seeing how Jesus affirmed the importance of loving the one true God with every aspect of ourselves, it behooves Christians to familiarize themselves with this important Jewish prayer. It is printed below for that purpose.

"Hear, O Israel: The LORD our God, the LORD is one. You shall love the LORD your God with all your heart and with all your soul and with all your might. And these words that I command you today shall be on your heart. You shall teach them diligently to your children, and shall talk of them when you sit in your house, and when you walk by the way, and when you lie down, and when you rise. You shall bind them as a sign on your hand, and they shall be as frontlets between your eyes. You shall write them on the doorposts of your house and on your gates" (Deuteronomy 6:4–9).

"And if you will indeed obey my commandments that I command you today, to love the LORD your God, and to serve him with all your heart and with all your soul, he will give the rain for your land in its season, the early rain and the later rain, that you may gather in your grain and your wine and your oil. And he will give grass in your fields for your livestock, and you shall eat and be full. Take care lest your heart be deceived, and you turn aside and serve other gods and worship them; then the anger of the LORD will be kindled against you, and he will shut up the heavens, so that there will be no rain, and the land will yield no fruit, and you will perish quickly off the good land that the LORD is giving you. You shall therefore lay up these words of mine in your heart and in your soul, and you shall bind them as a sign on your hand, and they shall be as frontlets between your eyes. You shall teach them to your children, talking of them when you are sitting in your house, and when you are walking by the way, and when you lie down, and when you rise. You shall write them on the doorposts of your house and on your gates, that your days and the days of your children may be multiplied in the land that the LORD swore to your fathers to give them, as long as the heavens are above the earth" (Deuteronomy 11:13–21).

"The LORD said to Moses, 'Speak to the people of Israel,

and tell them to make tassels on the corners of their garments throughout their generations, and to put a cord of blue on the tassel of each corner. And it shall be a tassel for you to look at and remember all the commandments of the LORD, to do them, not to follow after your own heart and your own eyes, which you are inclined to whore after. So you shall remember and do all my commandments, and be holy to your God. I am the LORD your God, who brought you out of the land of Egypt to be your God: I am the LORD your God'" (Numbers 15:37–41). [Please note that this third section is recited only in the morning when the *tallit* (garment with tassels) is put on.]

The first portion of the Shema asserts the oneness of God and the supremacy of His kingship, commanding people to love God with their whole selves and teach their children to do the same. The second portion shows how obeying these commands leads to rewards, but disobeying them leads to punishment. It also repeats contents of the first portion of the prayer, but this time it does so in second person plural, speaking to the whole community rather than just the individual. The third portion helps people fulfill these commands by wearing the *tzitzit* (tassels) as a visual reminder of their commitment to keeping their covenant with God.

Things like the *tzitzit* are part of the Mosaic covenant and not necessary for Christians today. But the Bible is the inspired Word of God, and all of it is profitable for helping us know God and for equipping us to live for Him (2 Timothy 3:16–17). Christians can look to the words of the Shema as a beautiful expression of God's kingship and covenant-keeping ways and as a call to live out a love for God that not only hears but also obeys His call to love Him and love our neighbors."

(James 1:22–25; John 15:1–17; 1 John 3:16–18, 23–24; 4:7–12). (Gotquestions.org)

For me, the Shema links directly back to the first commandment expressed in Deuteronomy 5, which says, *"You shall have no other gods before me."*

As I've mentioned before, the NASB (and other translations) render the word *before* as *besides*. I prefer that wording since it goes much deeper and extends much wider in terms of its theological implications.

The appropriation and application of this verse is rooted in the principle and practice of consecration. And, consecration is at the heart of a Biblically-based commitment to Christ and God's kingdom.

> *"Bless the Lord, O my soul, and all that is within me, bless His holy name."*
>
> ~Ps. 103:1

Ever wonder what the phrase "all that is within me" is intended to mean?
Selah (pause , ponder)

THEOLOGY: (Show Your Work)

There is a term used in the study of mathematics that I need to appropriate here. It's this: Show your work. It has to do with being able to explain how you solved a particular problem or developed a certain equation. What follows here is me showing my work as it relates to the theological topic of believers and disciples. In order to do so, I'm going to take what may seem like an unusual pathway. I'm going to present the process I've followed in my personal considerations of the possible diffraction between believers and disciples.

My questing has taken me down pathways that were sometimes distractions or sometimes dead ends. As a result of that, I've had to backtrack and make course corrections several times.

However, the end result has brought me to a place from which I have been able to recalibrate and continue my Kingdom sojourn.

Before I show you the work I've done, I'll address an approach to how I view the subject of personal theological development. Doing so may help you to track my progress along the roadway to Zion.

Open-Handed or Close-Fisted

I see two basic ways of possessing (owning) one's personal theology.

One is with an open hand. What I mean by that is that you carry your theological beliefs in the palm of your hand so to speak. When held that way, your beliefs are yours to own and share. They are solid and steady held in that fashion, while at the same time, they can be tested by others, or by circumstances, or even by the Holy Ghost. Held that way, they remain yours, but they are not fearful as to their worth or merit.

The other is in a closed fist. Held in that matter, beliefs are grasped tightly, and only sharable when one of two things takes place:

- You willingly open your fist so that your beliefs are exposed (accessible) to others
- Someone is able to pry them from your close-fisted hold.

One way is Christlike, and reflective of God's kingdom principles and precepts. The other isn't.

With that concept in mind, consider what comes next in this narrative.

Believers , Disciples (Discerning The Distinction)

To begin this section, I need to draw attention to the word *distinction*. *Distinct* does not mean *separate*. Think of a two-sided coin. Both sides are distinct from one another, but they are not separated. They are both joined together as one coin. Keeping that in mind will likely help you follow this unfolding narrative.

The terrain I'm about to head out into won't be an easy trek. There are rocks and boulders scattered all around, along with some hidden craters. There are several slippery slopes to navigate as well.

Nonetheless, the territory is part of my personal questing, so if you're gonna come along with me, you have been warned. Travel at your own risk.

For a fuller content, I'd like to examine two key words and their variations. They are essential to what's to follow:

- Believe (believed/believers/belief)—To have faith (in, upon, or with respect to, a person or thing.) To entrust one's spiritual well-being to Christ). To commit to, to trust.
- Disciple (disciples)—A learner or pupil.

Since a disciple is a student, a teacher is required for discipleship to take place. That is to say, a disciple would need someone to disciple them, a discipler. However, the word *discipler* isn't found in Scripture. The word for *teacher* is *Rabbi*, which means *teacher.*

So, a disciple is discipled by a teacher or a Rabbi. A disciple is under the tutelage of a teacher or Rabbi.

There are two basic theological perspectives regarding believers and disciples. One sees believers and disciples as being one in the same, with no distinction between the two titles (or categories).

The other sees believers and disciples as being two distinct groups of people.

If the first category mentioned above is correct, then nothing else really needs to be considered in that regard. However, if the second grouping is correct, the ramifications are huge. The musings that follow are intended to consider those dynamics, based on the possibility that believers and disciples are in fact two distinct categories of the redeemed.

NOTE: The content that follows has nothing to do with salvation. Believers and/or disciples are to be considered as being saved and "hidden with Christ in God" (Col. 3:1-4.)

DISCLAIMER: This narrative began taking shape some five years ago. It evolved into the form described here a year or so later. I included it in my first book entitled *Pondering(s)*, published in 2016. I'll be incur[oration it here because it still rings true for me in terms of content and intent.

PONDERING DISCIPLESHIP

*"And even when I am old and gray, O God, do not forsake me,
until I declare Your strength to this generation, Your power to
all who are to come."*

~Psalm 71:18 (NASB)

I love that verse. I started going gray when I was around eighteen years old, or thereabouts, so I can take some degree of ownership—a vested interest of sorts. But, I value it for another reason with considerably more attachment. I've been putting it into practice for almost forty years. Verses like the one above take on a much deeper and more urgent meaning once you've lived it out over several decades. Having just recently entered my seventieth year, my experiences with the principles and precepts of discipleship have grown into fairly long list. One of the advantages of aging, in terms of Kingdom service, is that you gain the ability over time to be able to look further back over your shoulder than those younger than you. That's a real asset when you are attempting to disciple the generations coming up behind you. That's the reason that the Scriptural directive regarding the joining of the generations retains such an important place in my life. It has for quite a spell.

There's another passage that I'll include here, because it speaks to the topic of this chapter in a profound way. Psalm 78:5-7 says:

*"He planted a witness in Jacob, set His Word firmly in Israel,
then commanded our parents to teach it to their children so the
next generation would know, and all the generations to come
know the truth and tell the stories so their children can trust
in God, never forget the works of God but keep His commands
to the letter."*

(MSG)

Some of us old-schoolers are still working it. We have a Biblically

mandate directly from Scripture to try our best to fulfill. This manuscript is part of that mandate.

"God doesn't come and go. God lasts. He's Creator of all you can see or imagine. He doesn't get tired out, doesn't pause to catch His breath. And He knows everything, inside and out. He energizes those who get tired, gives fresh strength to dropouts. For even young people tire and drop out, young folk in their prime stumble and fall. But those who wait upon God get fresh strength. They spread their wings and soar like eagles, they run and don't get tired, they walk and don't lag behind."
~Isaiah 40:28-31 (MSG)

Now that I've got that out of my system, I'll move along. Please try not to rush me.

Having made it to here in your reading, I compliment you. I trust the sojourning that's brought you this far has been worth the time and effort. I had given some thought to trying to find someone who could develop an app in order for folks to decipher "Wayne-Speak," but I abandoned that idea. Then I considered providing a link to the purchase of a decoder ring, but I gave up on that as well. I knew the Gen Xers and the Millennials would have no idea what such a thing was. So, you've been reading at your own risk. Now just keep pressin' ahead for a little further.

Since you're still with me I have a few words to say to you as encouragement. For some reason, the Holy Ghost has linked you and I together through the pages of this manuscript. So, it is not by chance that you're reading it. There is no such thing as *chance* in matters of God's kingdom. Divine happenstance perhaps, but chance?—Nada.

"And we know that God causes all things to work together for good to those who love God to those who are called according to His purpose."
~Romans 8:28 (NASB)

91

As I stated in the preface of this work, my intention has been to try and document my thoughts here on these pages so they would be available as a "sacrificial offering" for the Lord to use as He sees fit. I have no interest in trying to convince you to accept/believe anything I've written. Rather, I've tried to present some things to you for consideration in your own growth as a believer, or for your potential growth if/when you come to accept Christ as your Savior—the "hope of glory." (Colossians 1:27)

Some 25+ years ago, a book was published entitled, *This Present Darkness* that Christians all over the world were reading. The author, Frank Peretti, spoke at the church I was attending at the time, about a year or so after the book came out. He told a story about something that took place between himself and the Holy Spirit, which seems appropriate to share here.

He was in his study, sitting at his desk (as I recall), musing to himself, when this thought crossed his mind: "I've sold almost 750,000 copies of my book." At that moment the Spirit spoke to him and said, "Frank, you've written one. You've had nothing to do with how many books have been sold." As was the case with Frank, I've written one.

> *"We teach in a spirit of profound common sense so that we can bring each person to maturity. To be nature is to be basic. Christ! No more, no less. That's what I'm working so hard at day after day, year after year, doing my best with the energy God so graciously give me."*
>
> ~Colossians 1:28 (MSG)

Before I get into the subject of discipleship any further, I feel I need to stress this point one last time. The point of this manuscript isn't for me to persuade you to agree with what I'm sharing. How you process my ponderings is between you and the Holy Ghost. My purpose in trying to convey these things is to state my thoughts as clearly as possible. Any revelation or insight that you may garner

will have little to do with what I personally believe. How your belief system evolves will be based on how you sort thought the things the Lord places in your path.

Beyond that, I have no control over how these ponderings will affect your life, your theology, and your relationship to God's kingdom.

Discipleship: What It Is

I'll begin much in the same way I have in the previous chapters, by defining language and how it applies to specific words or concepts. In order to do that, the first thing to do is define the word *disciple* based on its common usages culturally and Biblically.

Webster's defines a *disciple* as one who accepts and assists in spreading the doctrines of another; a convinced adherent of a school or individual. Strong's Concordance defines it as a learner or pupil.

There is a perspective regarding how Christians understand some of the language used in Scripture, which is misleading. They tend to read the Bible in a context which appears to make every word in the Bible have a religious or spiritual meaning or intent. However, that is not the case. In both the Old and New Testaments, some of the wording that's presented has been taken from the culture in which it was spoken. In other words, each and every aspect of the wording isn't necessarily intended to carry a religious meaning. Some words certainly are meant to take on a spiritual intent when they are used in a spiritual context, but that doesn't mean that the words themselves are spiritual in nature. The word *disciple* is a perfect example of that. Let me explain it this way:

Within the culture that the New Testament was written, there were teachers who taught on many different subjects and beliefs. Those teachers had followers, or if you will, students who studied under their teaching. The concept of being a disciple was based on the role of a student learning under the tutoring of a qualified teacher. Think of that dynamic as applying to a classroom setting. There were students, and there were teachers. Based on the language of the day, the students would have been referred to as disciples,

and the teachers would have been their disciplers. The word *disciple* is found in Scripture, but the word *discipler* isn't. Nonetheless, it is implied anytime the word *disciple* is used, because in order to be a disciple there has to be someone who is discipling (teaching) their students. Also, just so you'll know, the word *discipleship* isn't in the Bible either. However, the role that a teacher (rabbi) would have fulfilled in Biblical times would have been to educate his disciples in the ways that they would have had to learn, in order to follow in the process of being discipled. That process would be called *discipleship*

There's another aspect to how Christians tend to understand the use of the term *disciple*. Because of how such a word (or role) is viewed from within the church-at-large, many believers think that when the word *disciple* is used, it is referring to the twelve disciples of Jesus. But, according to Scripture, that is clearly not the case. If the word *disciple* is used to specifically relate to one (or all) of the Twelve, then that is an appropriate interpretation. However, Jesus had many more disciples than the twelve we normally think of when the term is used. If you'll read Luke 6 for example, you'll find that He *called His disciples to Him and chose twelve of them"* (v.13). Hence, after choosing the Twelve from among an unknown number of His disciples, He then moved down the mountainside to where *"there was a large crowd of His disciples"* (v.17). Here we see Jesus first choosing His twelve from a group of disciples, and then His twelve, along with the group of disciples that the Twelve were chosen from, joining together to regather with an even larger group of disciples. The picture presented here shows us that Jesus as Rabbi (teacher) had a group of disciples (students) who were following His teaching—which is why and how they became known as His disciples. There is no place in Scripture where Jesus is credited with giving His disciples the name of *disciple*. That title would have been conveyed to them through an understanding of how the word *disciple* was used within the culture at the time that Scripture was documenting what was taking place.

NOTE: In John 8:31, Jesus doesn't call the Jews who had come

to believe His disciples. Rather, He tells them what would need to happen in order for them to become disciples. That is to say, He is not addressing them as such.

Without the background I've just stated, it is very hard to interpret the true role of a disciple in Scripture—which in turn makes it even harder to understand the role (and the term) in the times we live in currently. Hence, some theological misunderstanding has taken place over many years of misappropriation of the language we're presented with from Scripture.

Now, let's proceed—cautiously—to the heartbeat of this chapter by looking at how the position of a disciple today could perhaps be re-focused with a view toward a more sound, Biblically-based implementation.

Based on what I've just shared, I must make one more point of clarification regarding language as to how it's used—sometimes properly, and sometimes not.

Discipleship: What It's Not

As I've stated, the Biblical definition of *disciple* is a very simple one—a student (being taught by a teacher). The process in which that teaching takes place is called *discipleship*. For Christians, that is a proper use of the term for a student (disciple), and also the term for how a student is trained or educated (discipleship). However, there is another cultural term that has distorted the entire concept by substituting a word that is really only appropriate for use within a secular business or educational community. That word is *mentor*, or perhaps *mentorship*. Note please how that word is defined in Webster's, and note also where it originated:

MENTOR: A friend of Odysseus entrusted with the education of Odysseus' son Telemachus. A trusted counselor or guide; a tutor or coach.

The use of that term as a substitute for *discipleship* is not only unbiblical, it is also misleading in terms of its theological misappropriation. That's all I'll say about that.

For me, the subject of discipleship and the role of both a disciple (student) and a teacher (disciple) has a backstory, which led me to what I'm about to share next. The story is still unfolding as a work in progress Here's where I've come to so far.

The story begins in John 8:31-32 which reads:

> *So Jesus was saying to those Jews who had believed Him, "If you continue in My word, then you are truly disciples of Mine; and you will know the truth, and the truth will make you free.'*

Perhaps as far back as twenty years, I began sorting out that verse. I wasn't struggling with it, I just kept coming across it from time to time as I read and studied the Bible. I had the sense that the Lord was speaking to me through it, but I didn't exactly know how or why. Then, about ten years ago, I started looking at it with more attention. As I did, this is what I saw:

I noticed that Jesus was the one who was speaking. The Jews mentioned in the text had done nothing to engage Him in a conversation. In other words, Jesus had something to say to them that they hadn't brought up to Him for discussion. So, what He said was important enough to Him to bring it to their attention.

Then I noticed that the Jews mentioned were believers. I researched the word *believed* and found that it was the same word as *believe* in John 3:16 and in other passages as well.

The use of that word (in that context) wasn't saying that these particular Jews were coming to Jesus based on some aspect of mental interest or speculation. No, they had accepted Him as their Messiah—they were Kingdom converts. Finding that out heightened my interest in the text considerably.

I then saw the placement of certain conditional words within the text. Words that were either spoken, or implied as parenthetical. I started reading the passage this way:

> *"If you continue in My word, then you are truly disciples of*

Mine; and then you will know the truth, and then the truth will make you free."

~Jn.8:32 (emphasis added)

New light was now being shed on the verse that had been drawing me into itself for nearly two decades.

In light of that expanding illumination, I approached the verses from the perspective of what might have been the motivation for Jesus to make such a statement to believers who hadn't so much as asked anything about what He was saying. His comments were of His own doing. I assumed that He was trying to inform them of something they'd had no idea of, that had to do with their relationship with Him. It appeared to me that He was drawing them into a deeper aspect of intimacy that somehow went beyond merely being a believer.

At that point in my pondering, the Holy Ghost drew me directly back to the first two portions of verse 31. Christ had introduced a concept to these Jewish believers with a conditional word, meaning that they had a choice in regards to what He was about to say to them. He said *if* they would keep His word, *then* He would consider them to truly be His disciples. Jesus was clearly saying to these converts that there was a deeper place—another level—beyond where they currently were in their understanding and in their relationship to Him, and the things related to being His followers.

In Wayne-Speak, the implication of His words was this: "You believe in Me, and that's all well and good. But, there is a way of being with Me that you can take part in. To do so, however you will have to keep My word—obey what I tell you, follow My lead, yield to Me as *Savior and Lord* as you seek to know and fulfill My Father's will. "Then, following those stunning words, He went on to tell them that if they would do that, two more things would take place in their lives as believers.

1. They would come to know the truth.
2. Truth would set them freer than they already were by basic belief in Him.

You can be a believers without being a disciple, but you can't be a disciple without first being a believer.

After coming to a point of understanding which had taken years to arrive at, I accepted the fact that (according to Scripture) there are two distinctions or roles available through salvation in Christ Jesus. One is that of being a believer. The other is that of being a disciple. Having that settled in my head, I figured that was a perspective to carry and sort out for the rest of my life. However, that wasn't the end of the journey. It turned out to only be the beginning.

I began to notice that I rarely (if ever) heard this concept mentioned as it related to our lives in Kingdom service to Christ Jesus. I knew of no teachings or published works regarding what I believed that John 8:31-32 said, nor was I aware of any sermons which addressed this topic of believers and disciples. I decided the less said the better since the subject seemed to be one that I was perhaps misunderstanding entirely. And then, *Bam!* A book by Dallas Willard entitled *The Great Omission* ended up in my lap.

That's when this entire process got very interesting.

The premise of Willard's work in that book gave me a broader context in which to consider this business of believers and disciples. Very simply and briefly the overview is this:

Christ fulfilled two key roles while He was here on earth. He was the Messiah, the Savior of humankind. He was also a Rabbi. His Messianic role was accepted by those who gave their lives to Him as their Redeemer. The other role (that of Rabbi) was accepted within the culture of His day by everyone who knew Him to be a knowledgeable and qualified teacher, and also by those who decided to follow Him—by becoming His disciples—which is exactly what John 8:31-32 speaks to. Willard addresses this issue by titling his book, *The Great Omission* Here's what he means by that:

The contemporary church of today accepts Christ as Lord, and thereby enters into eternal life through the saving work of the Lord, receiving the promise of heaven and home. However, the acceptance

of Jesus as Rabbi (teacher/discipler) is no longer as important as it once was. At least not from a Biblically theological perspective. Why? Because for believers to accept Christ as their Rabbi, that would place them in the role of being a student (disciple) directly under His charge. By doing so, they would have to not only study and relate to what He teaches, but would then have to put into practice the things that are being taught. That process in and of itself has no real bearing on salvation, so consequently it has become a mere option in terms of how believers live out their lives in an intimate relationship of worship and service to their Savior and Lord. That is, as Willard calls it, The Great Omission—accepting Jesus as Savior, but (in a sense) rejecting Him as Teacher. This in turn makes becoming a disciple a non-essential in terms of how we as Christians live our lives.

Having read that, I now knew that there was at least one other person—considerably more knowledgeable than I—who related to this believer/disciple subject the way I did. If I was way off target about this, I knew I wasn't the only one.

Then this happened…

The "Great Commission"

About three years ago, I was in intercession for the nations (Psalm 2:8) when I began to pose a prayer to the Father. The prayer question was, "Lord, why is the charge of the so-called 'Great Commission' taking so long to be fulfilled?" When I prayed that, in my spirit I heard the Holy Ghost say, "Consider John 8:31 and 32."

I was stunned! From there, the interchange that took place turned into a profound moment in my life. I said, "What does the John 8 passage have to do with Matthew 28:18-20?"

The Spirit said, "Who did Jesus give the charge of the Great Commission to?" As I re-read the passage I noted that Christ had spoken it directly to His disciples. At that moment, the Spirit answered my original question by saying, "The reason that the

Great Commission is taking so long to be fulfilled is that there are too few disciples available to get the job done."

I was undone, overwhelmed, broken, and astounded. Up until that moment, I had understood/believed that the words Jesus had spoken in Matthew 28:18-20 were directed to and intended for the body of Christ at large. They were not. The only people present when the "Great Commission" was spoken were His disciples and their Lord.

> *"But the eleven disciples proceeded to Galilee, to the mountain which Jesus had designated. When they saw Him, they worshiped Him; but some were doubtful. And Jesus came up and spoke to them, saying, "All authority has been given to Me in heaven and on earth. Go therefore and make disciples of all the nations, baptizing them in the name of the Father and the Son and the Holy Spirit, teaching them to observe all that I commanded you; and lo, I am with you always, even to the end of the age."*
>
> ~Matthew 28:16-20 (NASB)

The links between John 8:31 and 32 to the writings of Dallas Willard in *The Great Omission,* and then on to the words Jesus spoke directly and specifically to His disciples in Matthew 28:16-20, had all fallen into place. The Holy Ghost answered my question regarding the fulfillment of the charge Christ gave. He (the Spirit) also opened up an entirely different way of viewing the roles of believers and disciples.

My comments are not intended with a view toward some sort of class system among "born again" believers and disciples. There is no condescension contained in my remarks. One role is not above the other. There is no over/under position reference in Scripture, nor am I making any such claims. I am merely pointing out what I understand the passages I've mentioned to be saying. I am also explaining what has taken place in my belief system through my

interchanges with God's Word, and the moving of the Holy Ghost in my relationship with Him.

My bottom line is this: Jesus made a distinction between believers and disciples in John 8:31-32. Jesus spoke the so-called "Great Commission" to His disciples. He didn't do so by first separating or dismissing those who believed in Him. However, there is no mention of believers being present when the charge to the disciples to go make other disciples was spoken. That's because believers can't disciple others into becoming disciples. Only those who have been discipled by their teacher (Rabbi) are qualified and equipped to do that. As I said earlier, you can be a believer without being a disciple, but you can't be a disciple without first being a believer. That in turn, brings us full circle and returns us to the John 8:31, 32 text in Jesus' own words to believers.

The key that unlocks each of those doors is, *"if you keep my word,"* not *"are you saved?"* Those are two entirely different statements. One has to do with salvation, the other has to do with unconditional and obedient service. There's a term for that—it's *consecration*.

Pentecost to the Present:

There is one remaining bridge to be crossed regarding the subject of discipleship. It's found in Acts 1:8 as a link to the "Great Commission" and the role of believers and disciples.

> *"You will receive power when the Holy Spirit has come upon you; and you shall be My witnesses both in Jerusalem. And in all Judea and Samaria, and even to the remotest part of the earth."*
> ~Acts 1:8 (NASB)

As was the case when Jesus gave His charge to "go and make disciples" to the eleven disciples who were with Him, so also the comments (the directives) of Acts 1:8 are spoken to disciples.

I'll address how the impartation of Acts 1:8 applies to *all* Christians shortly. But, for now just consider what I'm about to say in

the context of what was taking place just prior to Pentecost among disciples only. Why? Because no believers are mentioned in that verse, so we are given no record that believers were in attendance. Nothing tells us that they were excluded for any reason. However, there is no record of anyone being present to receive what was spoken except for disciples.

You may recall that in the chapter focused on Presence, I mentioned a protocol for how a theology of omnipresence evolved from the answer to Moses' prayer in Exodus 33:13-17. Now, apply that protocol to the Acts 1:8 unfolding.

The passage clearly states that the Power of the Spirit is preceded by the impartation of Presence.

> *"You shall receive power after the Holy Ghost has come."*
> ~Acts 1:8 (emphasis added)

The verse goes on to say what will happen thereafter. Once empowered by the Spirit (after Presence has come), the disciples will become witnesses. The text doesn't say that they will go and do witnessing. It says that they will become witnesses themselves. Their lives will be transformed by the indwelling Power of the Spirit through the internal Presence abiding inside of them. That is exactly what Moses prayed for, and that is exactly how Jehovah said He would answer Moses' prayer!

The prayer of Exodus 33:13-17 was that God's Presence would go with His people so that they would be known (set apart) through such Presence in order that anyone and everyone they would come in contact with would know that they were in fact God's chosen people (1 Peter 2:9). Moses stated that just having God's living Presence would be enough to "distinguish" them from those who didn't know the One True God.

He didn't say that God's people would have to *do* anything. He said they would only have to show up with God's Presence abiding in and among them. Doing so would in turn make them witnesses—which is what Acts1:8 says what the disciples would become in order for them to carry out the remaining directive of that verse. They were to go out into the regions of the world as witnesses and proclaim their testimony, which produces Kingdom expansion as conversions took place. Then, once souls had been redeemed through the saving grace of God working through the drawing of the Spirit, the ability for the disciples to make more disciples would be possible.

The cycle of answered prayer for Presence, which began in the interchange between Moses and Jehovah, continued all the way to the charge of the "Great Commission." This in turn is directly linked to the charge of the pre-Pentecost directives of Acts 1:8. And, the outworking of the Acts 1:8 mandate (for all intents and purposes) falls directly in line with Moses' requests and Jesus' statement to His disciples in Matthew 28:16-20. The *"Go ye"* (KJV) is the call that was given. That call began with Moses' prayer, and then finds its way into the ears (and hearts) of the disciples—both then and now. That process brings us to how it applies to ALL believers living today, and those believers who are yet to be "born again" into active service for the expansion of God's kingdom.

SPLENDOR

The charity of God's Spirit
Is a gift beyond all measure
It's a treasure that can't be bought or sold
The Holy intervention
Of His Presence here among us
Creates a world of wonders to behold

Encounters in His kingdom
For those with eyes to see them
Are expressions of a life meant to be shared
Like an every-flowing fountain
Running down from off Mount Zion
Freely pouring out to everywhere

Still You move, on the wind
Over and over again
Still You move in splendor

The clarity of purpose
Manifest through grace, through mercy
Can be measured day to day without an end
As the hope sent down from heaven,
Touches every generation
The cycle is repeated once again

Still You move, on the wind
Over and over again
Still You move in splendor

~W. Berry, See & Say Songs, BMI

The Son asks the Father to send the Spirit to teach converts (John 14:26) how to become worshippers of the One True God (Deuteronomy 5:7) in "spirit and in truth" (John 4:23). As we grow in our understanding of how to live a lifestyle of covenantal consecration, we are then equipped to serve the Lord as His witnesses (Acts 1:8), by giving testimony to who He is in our lives. In doing so, we become pro-active in our role as ambassadors for Christ, extending the gift of reconciliation to all those who will be added to the church in order to advance the kingdom (2 Corinthians 5:18-21).

THE BIG IF

> *"Life is meant to be lived from a Center, a Divine Center. Each one of us can live such a life of amazing power, peace and serenity of integration and confidence and simplified multiplicity, on one condition—that is, if we really want to."*
>
> ~T. Kelly

> *"If you keep my word..."*
>
> ~John 8:31-32

In the KJV translation, that phrase reads, "if ye continue in my word..." The word *continue* in the Greek is *meno*, meaning to stay (in a given place, relation or state of expectancy); to abide, dwell, endure, be present, remain, tarry (for or with). If that doesn't speak directly to an intimate relationship to Presence, then I don't know what does.

The qualifier for becoming a disciple is the keeping of God's word. Not belief in Jesus Christ as the Messiah. Not being "born again." Not good works, or the ability to perform "signs and wonders." Not evangelism. Not soul winning. Not mission work, or church planting. Living a lifestyle that testifies to obedient service by keeping God's word is the condition put forth in John 8:31 for

being a disciple of the Lord Jesus. How we understand, relate to, and embrace that one short phrase of Scripture is the determining factor for living as a disciple. The charge of the so-called "Great Commission" is incorporated into such a keeping of the Word. So is the empowerment imparted (to the disciples) in Acts 1:8. The going forth in order to make disciples is charged to those who are first disciples themselves.

> *"And do not be conformed to this world, but be transformed by the renewing of your mind, so that you may prove what the will of God is, that which is good and acceptable and perfect."*
> ~Romans 12:2 (NASB)

> *"The unspiritual self, just as it is by nature, can't receive the gifts of God's Spirit. There's no capacity for them. They seem like so much silliness. Spirit can be known only by spirit—God's Spirit and our spirits in open communion. Spiritually alive, we have access to everything God's Spirit is doing, and can't be judged by unspiritual critics. Isaiah's question, "Is there anyone around who knows God's Spirit, anyone who knows what He is doing?" has been answered: Christ knows, and we have Christ's Spirit."*
> ~1 Corinthians 2:14-16 (MSG)

RENEW MY MIND
(Rom. 12:2)

Sometimes I'm feelin' down so low, I just can't face the day
The tempters turned my heart so cold,
and heaven seems so far away
But then I see where I've gone wrong,
I've strayed away from You too long
I long to be where I belong,
so down on my knees I pray
Heavenly Father, help me find my way

CHORUS:
Father, renew my mind
set my thoughts in the heavenlies
Father, I've been so blind,
now I need the touch of Your hands on me
Father, open up my eyes,
let me see what You are doing
I'm willin' just to be a part,
of how Your Holy Spirit is moving
Father, renew my mind,
Father, renew my mind
Heavenly Father, renew my mind

As a child of God I'm called to live,
a life of love and grace
To give all that I've got to give,
until I behold His face
But, sometimes sin takes hold of me,
it won't let go, and I can't get free
But my sweet Savior rescues me,
and every demon has to run
At the power in the name of God's Son

REPEAT CHORUS:

~W. Berry, See & Say Songs, BMI

Some say that the organized church is in decline in America. That may be the case, but, I know from personal experiences (12 years of ministry on the continent of Africa), that it is exploding and expanding there as well as in nations all over the earth (see Psalm 2:8). Conversions into God's kingdom are taking place in huge numbers. Belief in Christ is increasing at a steady and rapid rate. However, there continues to be a shortage of disciples in fellowships large and small. The wooing of the Spirit, drawing millions into redemption through Christ Jesus, is taking place unabated. But, the call for disciples who are willing and equipped to make disciples is lacking in congregations everywhere (Matthew 28:19).

Coming to terms with that reality could create perhaps the greatest display of Presence, Power, and Proclamation for the kingdom of God that humankind has ever known. We, as God's people—the chosen and elect (I Peter 2:9)—continue to be grace-favored with the opportunity before us to see that "*the earth will be filled with the knowledge of the glory of the Lord, as the waters cover the sea*" (Habakkuk 2:14). That mandate awaits those who will hear the call, and yield themselves to it—through their ongoing acts of consecration, worship, and the empowerment of the abiding-indwelling Presence of God's Holy Spirit, going forth into "*all Judea, and Samaria, and even to the remotest part of the earth (Acts 1:8).*"

CLEAN, CLEAR

Over the last several years, I have written, taught, and publicly shared on the topic of believers , disciples. It has been a lengthy and intense theological struggle. I have finally reached a personal resolution that I think I should mention, in order to be clean , clear with anyone who might have been exposed to and/or influenced by my narratives on that subject. Although I don't consider John Piper to be *the* authority on the subject under consideration, I do think his explanation is perhaps as concise as any I've come across.

Having said that, Piper's perspective has offered me a place to park, so to speak.

Listen if you choose. Apply his comments if they seem appropriate. And then, continue to "press on toward the goal for the prize of the upward call of God in Christ Jesus." (Phil.3:14)

MAKING DISCIPLES

A couple of observations about the word *discipleship*. The word *discipleship* never occurs in the Bible. The term is ambiguous in English. It can mean my discipleship, in the sense of my own pattern of following Jesus and trusting him and learning from him. That is my discipleship. It could mean that. Or it can mean my activity of helping others be disciples in that sense of learning from him, growing in him.

People need to become Christians, and people need to be taught how to think and feel and act as a Christian. That is a disciple.

The second meaning—*helping others*—does have a verb in New Testament Greek: *mathēteuō*, to make disciples. It can mean preach the gospel so that people get converted to Christ and become Christians and, thus, disciples. For example, Acts 14:21 says, "When they had preached the gospel to that city and made many disciples, they returned to Lystra and to Iconium." So that "make disciples" is one Greek word there, and it means "get them converted to Jesus." That is what it means.

Or it can mean the whole process of conversion, baptism, and teaching the ways of Jesus as it is used in Matthew 28:19–20: "Go therefore and make disciples." And here is what he means. "Baptizing them in the name of the Father and of the Son and of the Holy Spirit, teaching them to observe all that I have commanded you."

That is a very long process. That is like a lifetime of process. So get them converted. Baptize them. And then spend a lifetime teaching them to obey all that Jesus said. That is what the verb "disciple" in the New Testament would include.

Second-Stage Christians

The word *disciple* in the New Testament does not mean a second-stage Christian. There are some ministries that are built around this distinction that is just so unbiblical, as if there were converts, then there are disciples who are little stage-two Christians who learn more, and then there are disciple makers.

Now all those groupings are linguistically foreign to the New Testament. A disciple in the New Testament is simply a Christian: "And in Antioch the disciples were first called Christians" (Acts 11:26). Everybody that was converted to Jesus was a disciple. Everybody that was converted to Jesus was a Christian.

Disciple was, it seems, not a favorite term for *Christian* as time went by. Paul never uses the noun or the verb "disciple." In fact, neither the noun *disciple* or the verb *make disciples* occurs anywhere in the New Testament outside the Gospels and Acts.

So I think what is important is not the terminology, but the reality. People need to become Christians and people need to be taught how to think and feel and act as a Christian. That is, a disciple, a follower of Jesus, one who embraces him as Lord and Savior and Treasure.

How To

Now where and how should that happen? That is what I think all the talk about discipleship is. It's a fresh concern about how to bring people to Christ and grow them up into being what they ought to be as Christians or as followers of Jesus or as disciples. There is a lot of different words that people are using these days to describe "Christian."

So how does that happen?

Well, the conversion of people from unbelievers to believers, Christians, disciples, should be happening in any and every situation. There is no single strategy. There is no limit to the ways a

person can be told the good news of Jesus. So, "discipling" in that sense is as varied as there are ways of saying the gospel or living the gospel in front of people to draw them in.

As far as training Christians how to think and feel and act as a Christian—that is, discipling in the sense of growing them into more and more maturity—that happens in so many ways in the New Testament. Here is just a grocery list of possibilities:

- Titus 2:4—Older women are to train younger women.
- Second Timothy 2:2—Paul trained Timothy to train others to train others.
- Ephesians 6:4—Fathers are to train their children.
- Matthew 28:20—Missionaries are to teach the nations everything Jesus commanded.
- Hebrews 3:13—All Christians are to exhort each other every day to avoid sin and to stir each other up to love and good works (see also Hebrews 10:24–25).
- First Peter 4:10—All Christians are to use their gifts to serve others.
- Acts 18:24–26—Priscilla and Aquila, on the spur of the moment it seems, explained the way of God more accurately to Apollos.

And we could go on and on.

Every Christian should be helping unbelievers become believers by showing them Christ. That is making a disciple. And every Christian should be helping other believers grow to more and more maturity. That is making a disciple.

And every Christian should be seeking to get help for themselves from others to keep on growing. And that is also our discipleship. And every church should think through how all of these kinds of biblical disciple-making find expression in their corporate life.

This quote is where I've currently determined to settle myself (and my theology) in regards to the subject at hand:

"What is important is not the terminology, but the reality."

~John Piper

That thought lines up with something that the Holy Ghost showed me over a decade ago.

It has to do with what in retrospect was likely an early prompting about recalibration. Here's what happened:

I had been trying to process how to deal with a number of issues related to humanity-at-large, global conditions (environmental / political , spiritual). How should I pray through? What should my intercessory focus be? How do I burden bear for others? Is the practice of lament something I should research more deeply and then apply more directly?

While attempting (over time) to sort all that out, The Spirit directed my attention to Psalm 131 which says,

"O Lord, my heart is not lifted up;
my eyes are not raised too high;
I do not occupy myself with things
too great and too marvelous for me.
But I have calmed and quieted my soul,
like a weaned child with its mother;
like a weaned child is my soul within me.
O Israel, hope in the Lord from this time forth and forevermore."

That in turn led me to the Charles Spurgeon commentary on that text from *The Treasury Of David*. I encourage you to take the time to go to the link below and read what Spurgeon has to say.
https://www.desiringgod.org/interviews/what-is-discipleship-and-how-is-it-done

The essence of what I've found in my seeking for clarity about all this is that peace and centeredness is best achieved by coming to terms with God's Sovereign control. The things I don't/can't understand (or fix) are best left in His divine care. My charge in such situations is to learn how to leave certain things as they are, and just rest (in hope, by faith) in His ability to sort things out.

Section Four
THE PARTICIPATION

CITIZENSHIP (BIRTHED RIGHT)

"But our citizenship is in heaven."

~Phil. 3:19, 20

"The word translated as "citizenship" is *politeuma*, a word that is better translates as "commonwealth" or "colony." It means a politically organized body with laws and loyalties that govern the behavior of its citizens. Literally it tells Christians that their politics—the way they conduct themselves in society—is to be based on the life of heaven...the church is an alternate society, not simply a collection of individuals who are forgiven. It is a "holy [distinct, set apart] nation" (1 Peter 2:9), a counterculture, a new society in which the world can see what family dynamics, business practices, race relations, and all of life can look like when the Spirit begins to heal all the effects of sin: psychological, social, and physical. In this sense the church must follow God's standards and directives and laws rather than the world's, and it shows the world what a new humanity should be."

~Tim Keller

THE MINISTRY OF RECONCILIATION

In order to reach unity of purpose and agreement, the processing principle of reconciliation is required. The first step in that process is to define what reconciliation is. And, most people—inside or outside the church—don't have a biblical understanding of what it is. That's because it hasn't been clearly explained within the context of our corporate/congregational gathering. As a result, those who follow Christ have the same basic (temporal) concept of reconciliation as those who don't. Everybody thinks the process is about compromise.

Generally speaking, we tend to believe that reconciliation means that two (or more) people have differing opinions or beliefs as to how to come together in some form of unity. That concept is supposed to work by each "side" giving up some portion of their position to meet the other person (or persons) "half way." That is a form of reconciliation, but it is not the biblical form.

If you read 2 Corinthians 5:18-21, you'll find the dynamics of *reconciliation presented there in black and white. In that context, reconciliation isn't based on two (or more) coming together through compromise. Nope, that the cultural, social, or political way it's done. However, the scriptural meaning is to take two (or more) positions, opinions, or beliefs and *combine* them into a compound or substance that didn't exist before they were combined. That is to say, the end result of combining (reconciling) things together in turn creates something altogether "other" from what there was to begin with. That process has a name—it's called *reconciliation*.

Here's an example that may better explain what I've said:

Suppose you want to paint a room in "Unity Blue," which isn't available as a pre-mix. You show the paint salesperson a swatch with the color you want, and then they go to work mixing "other" colors together. There may be more than two colors needed. In fact, there may be several different and distinct colors necessary to get the color you want. Most often, they are all added to a base

color of white, like a blank canvas. Each color is mixed together, with whatever percentage is required. A little of some, more of the others. Once all the colors are in the mixture, the entire can is sealed and shaken in order to form a color that wasn't available until they were combined together.

Now, consider this: Once all the colors have been combined (reconciled), they can never be separated back to their individual colors. Why? Because each individual color has become one collectively. That process also has a name—it's *unity*!

Reconciliation, In Greek: (Katallagay')—To exchange through adjustment. Restoration (to divine favor). From (Katallas'so)—Meaning to change mutually, to compound from a difference.

Selah (pause, ponder)

Here are two examples of reconciliation:

1. Jesus was fully Divine, but He willingly became human in obedience to the Father's request (Phil. :5-10). Consider the Divine aspect as part A of the equation of reconciliation. Then, consider humanity as part B. Compounded together, a Being that had never existed came to life. Life, temporal when He died on the Cross. And, life eternal, when He was resurrected. Now, He lives eternally making intercession for the saints (Heb. 7:25). That, dear cohorts, is *ongoing reconciliation in action.*

2. When a man and a woman are wed, Scripture says they become "one." Man is part A, and woman is part B. Together they form a unit (or unity) of reconciliation that didn't exist prior to their joining. They are to remain such until parted by death.

Now, consider both of those examples in light of what 2 Corinthians 5:18-21 says regarding the ministry of reconciliation (job description), and ambassadorship for Christ (job title).

I think what follows here is pretty important:

Regarding point #1: The general understanding that reconciliation has to do with two opposing positions being reconciled by one (or both parties) compromising doesn't apply. That process is based on a give-to-get dynamic. A sort of trade-off if you like. In

relation to how the ministry of reconciliation works between the Father and Son, there is no such interchange involved. Here's why:

2 Corinthians 5:19 says that "God was in Christ reconciliation (reconciling) the world (humanity) to Himself, not counting their trespasses (our sin) against them (us)." Emphasis added.

That took place *prior* to "The Garden, The Fall," in eternity past. There were no humans on earth at variance with Jesus. The "trespasses" (sins) of *all* humankind hadn't taken place when God placed the ministry of reconciliation in Jesus—it was there before the process of Creation had even begun. Therefore, what Jesus brought with Him to earth was forgiveness of sin(s) before the first sin had taken place. That is to say, God in Christ activated reconciliation, not counting *our* trespasses! That is the Biblical perspective on the very ministry we're given when we enter into a redemptive relationship with Christ Jesus. (See Col. 3:1-4.)

Regarding point #2: The man and woman (about to wed) aren't considering any disagreement or separation between them. At least they shouldn't be. They are "in love," so their objective is to join themselves in "holy matrimony." Again, we see that the better way of understanding reconciliation isn't to get past some sort of disagreement or conflict. Rather, it is to be proactive about taking an action that can create/form a compounded substance out of two different things. A + B = C.

Selah (pause , ponder)

RECONCILIATION: To exchange or adjust; to release divine favor*. From a word meaning to change mutually; to compound a difference. From a word meaning to join together. From a word meaning to make different by change.

*Keep in mind that divine favor can be understood as grace. (See Heb. 4:16.)

Time Management

Time is a construct, created by God to frame (contain) human history, along with everything else that takes place on the earth.

Since eternity is not bound by earth-time as such (having no beginning or ending), time's earthly framework has no direct bearing on what takes place in eternity. Eternity was, is, and will be. Earth-time only exists to provide a container for events which have happened, are happening, and will happen on this planet in the future. Eternity does not respond to earth-time as such, since it takes place outside of it. Now, I'll try to unpack that a little.

> *"In the beginning..."*
>
> ~Gen. 1:1 (NASB)

In the matter of time, the most important word in that phrase from Genesis 1:1 is *beginning*. Here's why. God was moving from within eternity (which has no beginning) to establish the very existence of *time* itself. He created it to provide a context for what He intended to do on the earth. During the act(s) of creation, He set in place a framework from which time could unfold. Day #1 and following presents us with a defined measurement. Regardless of what your personal perspective is concerning "creation theology," it is clear from Scripture that each day was measured by a specific construct of time—having both a beginning as well as an ending.

> *"From the rising of the sun, till it's going down..."*
>
> ~Ps. 113:3

Here are two Biblical statements that reflect the biblical history of how people have understood life in terms of time since it began: *"My times are in Your hand..."* (Ps. 31:15) and *"Teach us to number our days..."* (Ps. 90:12). Those are both Old Testament perspectives. The New Testament shares a similar POV when it says, *"while it is still called today..."* (Heb. 3:12-15 (MSG).

Here's another:

> *"But when the fulness of time had come, God sent forth His*

117

Son, born of a woman, born under the Law, so that He might redeem those who were under the Law, that we might receive the adoption as sons."

~Gal. 4:4

There are so many Scriptures which address the subject of time. But, for now, those four give us a foundation upon which to build our own theology regarding the subject of time—where it came from, why it was fashioned, and what to do with/about it until it ends. I'll come back to the Galatians 4:4 text again later to consider it in more depth.

To recap, simply stated: God created time to provide a context for what He intended to do on the earth. At least that's how I currently understand the subject being addressed.

Having said all that, a question arises that needs consideration. *After God created time, what did He then intend to do?* Scripture tells us:

"Let us make man in our image."

~Gen. 1:26

RELATIONAL UNITY

The Trinity is relational—The Father, Son, and Holy Ghost—Three in One. The interaction between those three Persons is total, complete, and inter-connected eternally. A case can therefore be made stating that relationships are a fundamental aspect of eternal life. Relationship(s) are not only inspired and modeled by the Trinity, they are also, perhaps, the fundamental reason that humankind came into being in the first place.

Consider Psalm 133 as it relates to the subject of unity:

"Behold how good and how pleasant it is for brothers to dwell together in unity! It is like the precious oil upon the head, coming down upon the beard, even Aaron's beard. It is like the dew of

Hermon coming down upon the mountains of Zion; for there the Lord commanded the blessing—life forever."

~(NASB)

The scripture above is filled with mystery which I cannot address. Nonetheless, I believe it to be true and Biblically sound

If the Trinity said, *"let us make man in our image,"* then it must (at its foundational base) be intended to establish interaction between man (humankind) and the Trinity. The establishment and unfolding of the very first relationship(s) between man (Adam , Eve) and the Creator is presented to us in Scripture beginning at the creation of man and continuing up until "The Fall." When sin entered the world, the plan for re-establishing a relationship between God and man was introduced (Rom. 5:12-21). That plan was reconciliation (2 Cor. 5:18-21), or if you prefer, the Gospel, the "Good News." That *plan* was already in place in the mind of God before it was ever introduced on earth. It was in eternity, outside of earth-time. Therefore, it is an eternal plan. That concept is also filled with mystery. Since God is Omniscient (having infinite awareness, understanding, and insight) He knew what was going to take place regarding "The Fall" prior to it happening. It did not alter His plan. Rather, it was set into motion within the context of time. **Selah (pause , ponder).**

> *"But when the fullness of the time came, God sent forth His Son, born of a woman, born under the Law, so that He might redeem those who were under the Law, that we might receive the adoption as sons. Because you are sons, God has sent forth the Spirit of His Son into our hearts, crying, "Abba! Father!" Therefore you are no longer a slave, but a son; and if a son, then an heir through God."*
>
> ~Gal. 4:4-7 (NASB)

"Paul urged us to be "eager to maintain the unity of the

Spirit…until we all attain to the unity of the faith and the knowledge of the Son of God…" (Eph. 4:3, 13). Christian unity is not unity in what we believe or what we know about Jesus. It is unity of the Spirit. I have close friends who are committed to doctrines I cannot agree with, but we experience unity in the Spirit. We have different ideas about how to "do church," but we both worship Jesus Christ, the Son of God. Unity of the faith and "mature manhood" (Eph. 4:13) are yet to come. Strive to maintain unity."

~Fount Shults

RELATIONAL DISCONNECT (THE EFFECTS OF "THE FALL")

Before I address the subject of reconciliation, I need to say something else about the kingdom of God. To do so, I'll focus on two concepts:

- **Principle:** A goal to achieve (as in trying to reach the top of a mountain)
- **Precepts:** The pathway(s) that can be taken to help reach an intended goal

NOTE: Any given principle intended to be reached can have more than one pathway toward accomplishment. But, each pathway must keep the specific goal in sight. (See Ps. 84:5 and note that the word *highways* is plural. Also see Isa. 12:3 and note that the word *wells* or *springs* is also plural.)

Stated simply, we can reach our goal (principle) by following the pathways/streams (precepts) that will lead us there.

Now, stay with me here, this slope gets a little slippery: If the goal (principle) we're trying to reach is to live in and help establish/expand God's kingdom, *"on earth as it is in heaven"* (Mat. 6:10), then each and every pathway (precept) presented to us in Scripture is there to lead us directly to our goal. The catch is that we must do two key things to reach our goal.

- Learn what the precepts are
- Learn to follow the pathway(s) in obedience to the desired destination (principle)

If we choose to take other paths which lead us away from those presented in Scripture, we will end up off course, missing our intended goal. That's exactly why conviction, confessing, repentance, restoration, renewal, and (wait for it) reconciliation are all made available to us as followers of Christ. They provide co-ordinates [coordinates] for our GPS (Gospel Positioning System). Precepts of conviction, confession, repentance, restoration, renewal and reconciliation are all given to us to help us reach our goal—life lived in and of the Kingdom. I hope I didn't lose you somewhere along this trail.

> *"And how blessed all those in whom you live, whose lives become roads you travel; they wind through lonesome valleys, come upon brooks, discover cool springs and pools brimming with rain! God-traveled, these roads curve up the mountain, and at the last turn—Zion! God in full view!"*
>
> ~Ps. 84:5-7 (MSG)

An Axiom:
- Vision—Where we're going
- Mission—How we intend to get there
- Goal(s)—Markers along the way which help to determine progress (or lack thereof)

Vision should be progressive, not static. Mission is there to serve the vision. When there is no vision to pursue, mission becomes self-serving, and goals become useless.

> *"If people can't see what God is doing, they stumble all over themselves; But when they attend to what he reveals, they are most blessed."*
>
> ~Pro. 29:18 (MSG)

Reconciliation (On Purpose)

I'm not going to go into lengthy detail as to the meaning and implications of reconciliation. You can do that on your own time, and at your own pace. What I'll do here is focus in on the main text that I believe deals with the subject at hand.

> *"Now all these things are from God, who reconciled us to Himself through Christ and gave us the ministry of reconciliation, namely, that God was in Christ reconciling the world to Himself, not counting their trespasses against them, and He has committed to us the word of reconciliation. Therefore, we are ambassadors for Christ, as though God were making an appeal through us; we beg you on behalf of Christ, be reconciled to God. He made Him who knew no sin to be sin on our behalf, so that we might become the righteousness of God in Him."*
>
> ~2 Cor. 5:18-21 (NASB)

Here are the target points:

The plan of Reconciliation was created by the Father, passed on to the Son, and thereafter imparted to those who are "with Christ in God" (Col. 3:1-3), having been reconciled to the Father through Jesus (See 2 Cor. 5:18).

The plan of Reconciliation was formulated in eternity. It has been active on earth—in earth-time—since Jesus brought it with Him. But, *it is not time bound.* It is an eternal principle established to have no end.

The plan has only one pre-condition for it to become effective in someone's life. It must be accepted (received). In other words, the entire human race has the potential to be reconciled through union with Christ Jesus. (See Rom. 10:13.) The work to put that in place has already been completed (Jn. 17:4 , 19:30). All that's required for anybody/everybody to secure reconciliation is to take/receive it as their own. There are no other requirements. No class system issues or exclusions. No race restrictions. No color barriers.

No secret code. No nationalistic birthrights to present as documentation, etc. (See 2 Cor. 5:19.)

Anyone who is serving as an ambassador for Christ by extending the "ministry of reconciliation" to humanity-at-large must do so by placing no restrictions on anyone that is not mentioned in verse 19. If reconciliation is offered with the proviso that *some restrictions may apply*, then that ministry isn't the same as what Jesus imparts to those who follow Him. (The implications of this point are huge within the body of christ. We are missing this point big time!)

One of the keys which explains why all this is taking place is found in Hebrews 2:10 which says:

> *"For it was fitting for Him, for whom are all things, and through whom are all things, in bringing many sons to glory, to perfect the author of their salvation through suffering."*

That verse (as I understand it) builds a bridge which extends retroactively back to "The Fall." It tells us why man was created (to establish relationship), how that relationship was broken (through the sin of disobedience), who became the agent to reach across the divide through reconciliation (Christ Jesus), and how to accomplish what the Trinity intended to bring to pass from the moment that "let us make man in our image" was uttered. The objective has been, is now, and will always be to "bring many sons to glory."

In closing, I'll reinforce two things by mentioning them again:

According to 2 Corinthians 5:18-21 each/every follower of Christ has two things in specific that they are charged with.

They are given the "ministry of reconciliation" to offer/extend to *everyone* in direct accord with how it was given to us through Jesus from God. That is the job assignment of *every individual christian.*

The job title of *every individual christian* is to serve God's kingdom as an "ambassador of Christ."

The body of Christ is filled to overflowing with so-called believers who don't have a clue what either of those two points means, or how to

apply them to the life of service they say they are offering to the Lord.

Now, begin to process that as the Holy Ghost leads you, remaining open to fresh revelation in that regard.

An Axiom:

Revelation leads to Transformation and Transition leads to Impartation.

Selah (pause, ponder)

CHRIST'S FAMILY DNA

> *"In Christ's family there can be no division into Jew and non-Jew, slave and free, male and female. Among us you are all equal. That is, we are all in a common relationship with Jesus Christ. Also, since you are Christ's family, then you are Abraham's famous 'descendant,' heirs according to the covenant promises."*
> ~Gal. 3:28 (MSG)

> *"The Messiah has made things up between us so that we're now together on this, both non-Jewish outsiders and Jewish insiders. He tore down the wall we used to keep each other at a distance. He repealed the law code that had become so clogged with fine print and footnotes that it hindered more than it helped. Then he started over. Instead of continuing with two groups of people separated by centuries of animosity and suspicion, he created a new kind of human being, a fresh start for everybody."*
> ~Eph. 2:14, 15 (MSG)

> *"...work] out your own salvation with fear and trembling."*
> ~Phil. 2: 12 (NASB)

First, consider the context of the Philippians 2:12 text. It is written to a collective of believers, not to individuals. That is to say the "your" isn't a charge directed toward an individual. The singular aspects of the narrative are included in the corporate grouping. In

other words, Paul is saying that *we* should work out *our* salvation in and among other believers. The entire focus of the chapter has to do with what can best be called "body life." The group is the context in which the individual is to "work out" their salvation. Understood that way, the directive can be seen from an entirely different perspective than most contemporary followers of Christ relate to. It is a personal charge given in a corporate setting.

That being said, consider this variation of the Galatians 3:28 text mentioned above:

Citizens of heaven (kingdom cohorts), are not called to live with considerations given to race, creed, or color. Nor to denominational divides, political polarizations, or the basic principles of personal pettiness.

It is a sad and sorrowful state of affairs to realize how deeply the body of Christ at large has allowed self-serving theology to become so distorted through partisanship and so-called tribal division. Functioning as so many followers of Christ do today, it's no wonder that Christianity has become a seemingly irrelevant topic of consideration within the secular (pagan) culture of these daze we live in. To a large degree, we have lost our spiritual distinctive(s), by allowing our service as "ministers of reconciliation" to become so distorted by divisiveness.

Behold how good...Ps. 133

One body...Eph. 2:16

Kingdom life should override the values and dispositions of the fallen/secular cultures we live in. We are called to represent an entirely "other" way of living as "ambassadors for Christ" (2 Cor. 5:18-21). Presently, we are doing a poor job of that. Our ability to be identified as a "chosen generation," a "royal priesthood" and a "holy nation" (1 Peter 2:9), has been impeded by divisiveness and derision.

> *Make every effort to keep the unity of the Spirit through the bond of peace.*
>
> ~Eph. 4:3

AMBASSADORSHIP FOR CHRIST

Here are two articles related to how an ambassador is to carry out their service to the nation [remove extra space] they represent. They provide some much needed [much-needed] insight as to how such a position is to be understood and undertaken in the discharge of duty.

Ten Essential Qualities of an Effective Ambassador for Christ

6 Oct, 2016 in Evangelism, Outreach / Pastor to Pastor by Candace Waggoner

Representing Christ today requires three basic skills. First, Christ's ambassadors need the basic **knowledge** necessary for the task. They must know the central message of God's kingdom and something about how to respond to the obstacles they'll encounter on their diplomatic mission.

However, it is not enough for followers of Jesus to have an accurately informed mind. Our knowledge must be tempered with the kind of **wisdom** that makes our message clear and persuasive. This requires the tools of a diplomat, not the weapons of a warrior, tactical skill rather than brute force.

Finally, our **character** can make or break our mission. Knowledge and wisdom are packaged in a person, so to speak. If that person does not embody the virtues of the kingdom he serves, he will undermine his message and handicap his efforts.

These three skills—knowledge, an accurately informed mind; wisdom, an artful method; and character, an attractive manner—play a part in every effective involvement with a nonbeliever. The second skill, tactical wisdom, is the main focus of my book *Tactics*.

If you are an attentive student, in a very short time you will develop the art of maintaining appropriate control—what I call "staying in the driver's seat"—in discussions with others. You will learn how to navigate through the minefields to gain a footing

or an advantage in conversations. In short, you will be learning to be a better diplomat—an ambassador for Jesus Christ.

An ambassador is . .

1. **Ready.** An ambassador is alert for chances to represent Christ and will not back away from a challenge or an opportunity.

2. **Patient.** An ambassador won't quarrel, but will listen in order to understand, then with gentleness will seek to respectfully engage those who disagree.

3. **Reasonable.** An ambassador has informed convictions (not just feelings), gives reasons, asks questions, aggressively seeks answers, and will not be stumped by the same challenge twice.

4. **Tactical.** An ambassador adapts to each unique person and situation, maneuvering with wisdom to challenge bad thinking, presenting the truth in an understandable and compelling way.

5. **Clear.** An ambassador is careful with language and will not rely on Christian lingo nor gain unfair advantage by resorting to empty rhetoric.

6. **Fair.** An ambassador is sympathetic and understanding toward others and will acknowledge the merits of contrary views.

7. **Honest.** An ambassador is careful with the facts and will not misrepresent another's view, overstate his own case, or understate the demands of the gospel.

8. **Humble.** An ambassador is provisional in his claims, knowing that his understanding of truth is fallible. He will not press a point beyond what his evidence allows.

9. **Attractive.** An ambassador will act with grace, kindness, and good manners. He will not dishonor Christ in his conduct.

10. **Dependent.** An ambassador knows that effectiveness requires joining his best efforts with God's power.

—Gregory Koukl, *Tactics: A Game Plan for Discussing Your Christian Convictions*. Learn how you can grow these qualities in *Tactics*.

https://blog.churchsource.com/10-essential-quali-ties-of-an-effective-ambassador-for-christ/

An Axiom:

Knowledge is Information / Understanding is Interpretation / Wisdom is Application

How to Conduct Ourselves as Ambassadors for Christ
by David F. Maas, *Forerunner*, January 2004

To the members of God's church in Philippi, the apostle Paul writes, "For our citizenship is in heaven" (Philippians 3:20). While some may spiritualize this fact away, Paul's words come across as literal and real to those who understand that God has called us out of this world (John 15:19) and trans-ferred us into His Kingdom (Colossians 1:13).

Having our citizenship in the Kingdom of God by defi-nition makes us aliens in the physical country in which we live. Like ambassadors of a foreign government, we cannot participate in the politics of another country, a practice that would distract us from our real spiritual goal. However, we realize that the apostle Paul has challenged us to be ambas-sadors for Christ: "Therefore we are ambassadors for Christ, as though God were pleading through us: we implore you on Christ's behalf, be reconciled to God" (II Corinthians 5:20).

Do we have what it takes to be ambassadors of Jesus Christ? Do any of us know what an ambassador is supposed to do, or how an ambassador should behave? Do we know how an ambassador is expected to interface with the various publics with which he comes into contact?

A REAL AMBASSADOR

I met my first ambassador about seventeen years ago in Pas-adena, California, when a fellow Ambassador College faculty

member introduced me to the Press and Cultural Consulate of Finland, Mr. Jaako Bergquist. I struck up an informal conversation with him, mentioning I had lived and taught in a Finnish community up in Moose Lake, Minnesota. Since the faculty member had previously told Ambassador Bergquist that I hosted a classical music program on KBAC, the college radio station, I also informed him that Jean Sibelius—a Finn—was my favorite composer.

A week later, my colleague and I were invited to a get-together at the consulate's home in Beverly Hills. I had no idea what to expect, but I counted it as an opportunity to learn a little bit more about the diplomatic community. Through this, as well as other later encounters, I gained a better insight on what an ambassador does. Subsequently, I have had several opportunities to talk with Dr. Zion Evrony, the Israeli Consul General to the Southwest Region, when he visited Longview and Tyler, Texas.

A consulate, incidentally, is a branch embassy headed by a Consul General and many junior consuls. The Israeli Consulate for the American Southwest region, for example, is based in Houston. Its service area includes Texas, Louisiana, Arkansas, Oklahoma, and New Mexico. It does not have the same kind of diplomatic immunity as the main embassy in the nation's capital, but it is a real branch of an embassy, carrying on the same business that an embassy does.

Consulates are found in every major city, conducting the business of the countries they represent within the regional spheres of influence of those cities. We might draw a parallel between the embassy of a foreign country and the churches of God (whose real citizenship and headquarters are in heaven). The main embassies of Finland and Israel are located in Washington, DC, but consulates are found in New York City, Chicago, Los Angeles, Houston, and a number of other major metropolitan areas.

We could consider one of God's embassies to be the head-quarters of one the churches of God with the leading pastor or evangelist serving as the Chargé d'Affaires or the Consul General. The branch consulates are the individual, outlying congregations with its members serving as junior consuls. Every baptized church member's home could be designated as a branch consulate for the Kingdom of God. Realizing that we are members of God's diplomatic corps, it is important to know how to behave as a diplomat.

The first thing that impressed me at the get-together was the humble and gracious attitude and manner of our host, Jaako Bergquist. Mr. Bergquist assumed the position of a humble servant or steward, looking after the interests of his country, as well as serving and helping people like me to learn more about his country and its culture. For example, when he learned about my classical music radio program, he asked me if I would like to receive some musical recordings. Later that week, I received a package of fifteen long-playing records containing the complete symphonic works of Jean Sibelius. We played these recordings many times over KBAC and KBAU.

Jaako Bergquist was not a glad-handed super-salesman for his country, but more of an accommodating steward practic-ing what the apostle Paul counsels us to observe in Philippians 2:4: "Let each of you look out not only for his own interests, but also for the interests of others." Accordingly, the Finnish diplomat did not seem to be self-interested in the least, but was always interested in supplying the needs of others, actively esteeming others more than himself (verse 3).

A CULTURAL REPRESENTATIVE

A member of the diplomatic community realizes his extreme vulnerability as a minority member of a majority alien culture. Whether we like it or not, that role fits all of us. In such a position, a diplomat must be circumspect in

all his words and activities, careful not to offend his hosts or bring disrepute upon his homeland.

I was amazed at how many of the qualifications of an elder or overseer Paul lists in I Timothy 3:1-7 that Jaako Berquist possessed, including hospitality, the ability to teach, having his home in tip-top order, and exercising temperance and self-control. Like a busy switch engine in the Union Pacific freight yard, the industrious ambassador constantly moved from guest to guest, linking people together with common interests. At one point during the evening, he made sure I became acquainted with the Program Director of KUSC, a classical music station run by the University of Southern California. Later, he introduced to me an elderly couple from Esko, Minnesota, who had lived close to the community where I used to teach.

He made available, but did not push, the culture of Finland, somewhat like the philosophy of the Hershey Chocolate Company, which at one time relied largely on goodwill and word of mouth to advertise its products.

Occasionally, we may be afforded opportunities to assist other church of God groups with a special need. Not long ago, a local minister was somewhat vexed by intruders from other groups attempting to persuade members of his flock about the Nisan 15 Passover. Sabbath.org—one of our church's websites—contains a series of abstracts on sermons that thoroughly examines the subject. After downloading and printing these sermon abstracts, I dropped them off at the local minister's office on my way home from work. I reassured him that I did not want to proselytize or steal sheep, but only wanted to provide resources to help him defend his flock. To what extent he used those documents or how deeply his curiosity was piqued, I do not know, but he expressed a great deal of gratitude for those resources, promising that he would bookmark our site.

Another of our websites, BibleTools.org, provides another non-threatening resource to the greater church of God and the world at large, providing a lavish smorgasbord of truth and choice spiritual meat for those starving for understanding. Just pointing people to these resources can be a diplomatic way of availing others of the culture of the Kingdom of God.

At the Consulate's get-together in Beverly Hills, there were gentle but ubiquitous reminders that we guests were at a Finnish party: abundant Finnish food, Finnish vodka, Finnish artwork, murals and paintings of Finnish lakes and forests—reminding me of northern Minnesota and of northern Wisconsin—Finnish books, and Finnish symphonic and folk music playing over speakers throughout the residence. I became extremely homesick for Suomi or Finland—and I am not even Finnish!

GRACIOUS SPEECH

Besides humility and hospitality, Mr. Bergquist demonstrated diplomacy and wisdom, speaking very circumspectly, carefully considering the consequences of what he said, extremely careful not to injure the feelings of others needlessly. Later, while comparing notes, my colleague mentioned that he never heard Jaako Bergquist or any other member of the diplomatic community let his personal feelings enter the discussion. He merely repeated the official position of his country.

Likewise, we junior consuls of the government of God need to keep our pet opinions to ourselves (or at least qualify them as our own pet opinions). However, we must be knowledgeable of God's Word on any given subject, being ready to give an answer (I Peter 3:15). In addition, our words must model the gracious speech of our Elder Brother, who in John 14:10 says, "The words that I speak to you I do not speak on my own authority; but the Father who dwells in Me does the works."

Without scriptural backing, our own opinions are largely useless hot air. Consequently, as diplomates of God's government, we must learn to submerge our own feelings, being quick to listen and slow to speak, reflecting Jesus' half-brother's admonition in James 1:19.

Give no offense, either to the Jews or to the Greeks or to the church of God [perhaps during the current scattering the most difficult task of all], just as I also please all men in all things, not seeking my own profit, but the profit of many, that they may be saved.

Paul's mentor in diplomatic skills, Jesus Christ, had earlier proclaimed, "Woe to that man by whom the offense comes!" (Matthew 18:7). Some of us have been past masters at creating offenses, being wise as doves and harmless as serpents! As Christ's ambassadors, we must repent of such behavior.

If we want to follow the example of the master diplomat, the apostle Paul, schooled under both Jesus Christ and Gamaliel, we should look at a significant encounter he had with the philosophers at Athens in Acts 17. To begin, Paul paid the Athenians a compliment: "Then Paul stood in the midst of the Areopagus and said, 'Men of Athens, I perceive that in all things you are very religious'" (Acts 17:22).

If we were to read between the lines, Paul might be saying, "You Athenians are to be commended for your devotion to spiritual things." The King James' rendering of "religious" as "superstitious" exposes the latter word as having undergone what linguists call semantic drift. In Shakespeare's day and King James' time, this word did not have the negative connotation as it does now.

From the context of this account, it is plain that the apostle Paul was not, as some theologians like to characterize him, a feisty, wrangling, argumentative hothead. The men of Athens, who vastly outnumbered Paul and loved a good philosophical debate, could have made short work out of any

know-it-all smart aleck. The apostle Paul was thus lavish in his compliments.

Throughout his ministry, he frequently resorted to diplomatic language. At one point, he acknowledged a cultural debt both to the Greeks and to barbarians (Romans 1:14). In addition to complimenting strangers, Paul continually sought out similarities he shared between him and other grouPs. In a conflict in which both the Sadducees and the Pharisees were breathing fire down his neck, Paul masterfully ingratiated himself to the Pharisees, reminding them that he and they shared the same view on the resurrection (Acts 23:6-8). Paul, to the right people, let it be known that he was a Roman citizen (Acts 16:37-39; 22:25-29).

COMMON GROUND

We also need to find common ground, not only with people in the other groups of the church of God, but with the world at large, emphasizing (like mountains) the things we agree upon and de-emphasizing (like molehills) the things we disagree upon.

In the process of finding common ground, we dare not compromise our core values or syncretize them with the world. We should instead practice more of what the late church of God minister, Sherwin McMichael, counseled, "You don't have to tell all you know." Oftentimes, keeping our traps shut is the most diplomatic behavior of all (Ecclesiastes 3:7; Lamentations 3:28-29; Amos 5:13).

In Acts 17:23, the apostle Paul deliberately builds a bridge of common understanding and similarity, referring to something the Athenians already understood:

For as I was passing through and considering the objects of your worship, I even found an altar with this inscription: TO THE UNKNOWN GOD. Therefore, the one whom you worship without knowing [a more proper rendering than "ignorantly," another word that has also undergone semantic drift] Him I proclaim to you."

Later, in verse 28, Paul again seeks common ground by quoting from their own literature: "For in Him we live and move and have our being, as also some of your own poets have said, 'For we are also His offspring.'"

The important thing to remember is that the apostle Paul started at the Athenians' current level of understanding, continually finding commonalities between himself and his audience upon which to build mutual understanding and foster growth. An ambassador skillfully demonstrates how his country and another's country share similar interests. As the late Rabbi Meir Kahane pointed out, an alliance is not so much built on friendship as on common interests.

To summarize, in successful diplomatic negotiating, points we agree upon must be stressed and any disagreements must be de-emphasized. An ambassador should never be a pushy salesman or a glad-handed public relations man. Whatever his rank in the diplomatic community, Ambassador, Consul General, Chargé d'Affaires, junior consul, envoy, or diplomat, he has the following characteristics:

1. He is a representative of another culture, another way of life.

2. In this capacity, he does not give his own opinions, but advances the positions of his home country.

3. He functions as a servant or steward, representing his country faithfully.

4. As such, he practices hospitality, courtesy, and graciousness.

Proverbs 13:17 reads, "A wicked messenger falls into trouble, but a faithful ambassador brings health." As faithful ambassadors of Christ, we ought to bring health, refreshment, and comfort to the people with whom we come into contact.

https://www.cgg.org//index.cfm/fuseaction/Library.sr/CT/ARTB/k/871/How-Conduct-Ourselves-as-Ambassadors-for-Christ.htm

CORRIDOR OF LIGHT

If I'm in a bad circumstance, with very few choices
Caught up in the chaos, and hearing strange voices
There's a path that I can take, it's a way for me to go
Down the corridor of light, there's a hand that I can hold

CHORUS:
When I'm liftin' up Jesus, when I'm liftin' up Jesus
When I'm liftin' up Jesus, I'm takin' demons down

Even at the end of the age, there's a promise I can claim
I can dignify my trials, when I call upon His name
Then in the middle of the warfare, or at the end of my rope
I'll see a corridor of light, where there's a glimmer left of hope

REPEAT CHORUS
We're movin' from glory to glory, from strength to strength
From one level to another, we're all done with unbelief
With our eyes of Zion, God's holy hill
We'll see the corridor of light, that shines, and always will
~W. Berry / See & Say Songs, BMI

CROSSING THE KINGDOM CAUSEWAY

"The creation itself will be liberated from its bondage to decay and brought into the freedom and glory of the children of God."
~Rom. 8:21

"All the effects of sin—all the decay—of the world will be healed. Not only will there be physical liberation from disease, aging, and death, but there will be social liberation from poverty, war, racism, and crime that infest our world now, as well as psychological liberation from the fear, guilt, shame, and despair that infect us now. All things will finally be mended, put fully right. We ourselves will be made new, but we will also receive a renewed world in which to live with Christ in our resurrected bodies."
~T. Keller

"The resurrection means that the liberating, repairing power of God is here now, through the risen Christ and his presence in our lives through the Holy Spirit. We have not been saved just to be safe, but saved in order to serve."
~I. Lillias Trotter
Parables of the Cross

The Way Across

Jehovah built an overarching expanse for anyone and everyone who will use it to cross over. It's a Kingdom causeway spanning all the way from just after "The Fall" to "The Second Coming." It ends at the "Final Judgment." From there, it opens onto a gateway into eternity. If I were to give it a name, I'd call it "The Time History Bridge."

The passage below tells us *how* it was built:

"...we see Jesus, after being made temporarily inferior to the

137

angels (and so subject to pain and death), in order that he should, in God's grace, taste death for every man, now crowned with glory and honor."

~Heb. 2:9 (Phillips)

It goes on to tell us *why* it was built:

It was right and proper that in bringing many sons to glory, God (from whom and by whom everything exists) should make the leader of their salvation a perfect leader through the fact that he suffered. For the one who makes men holy and the men who are made holy share a common humanity. So that he is not ashamed to call them his brothers, for he says: "change to double quotation marks]I will declare your name to my brethren; in the midst of the congregation I will sing praise to you."

~Heb. 2:10, 11 (Phillips)

When Jesus had finished praying, a disciple came to him on behalf of the other disciples. He requested that Jesus teach *them* how to pray. This was/is his response:

"And it came to pass, that, as he was praying in a certain place, when he ceased, one of his disciples said unto him, Lord, teach us to pray, as John also taught his disciples. And he said unto them, When ye pray, say, Our Father which art in heaven, Hallowed be thy name. Thy kingdom come. Thy will be done, as in heaven, so in earth..."

~Lu. 11:1, 2 (KJV)

The Lord, Christ Jesus, gave that prayer to his disciples—those who considered themselves to be his followers. It was for them, and for those who follow him now, today. Those who are questing after him, his kingdom and his righteousness. Such seeking should be at the top of our listing of priorities.

Closing:

Eugene Peterson's rendering of Romans 12:1, 2 continues to serve as a sort of directional beacon in regards to my spiritual sojourning. I suppose it could be considered as a baseline default setting from which I can reassess the road I'm on—or the course I'm taking as I move from "strength to strength" (Ps. 84:5-7) and "glory to glory" (2 Cor. 3:18).

> *So here's what I want you to do, God helping you: Take your everyday, ordinary life—your sleeping, eating, going-to-work, and walking-around life—and place it before God as an offering. Embracing what God does for you is the best thing you can do for him. Don't become so well-adjusted to your culture that you fit into it without even thinking. Instead, fix your attention on God. You'll be changed from the inside out. Readily recognize what he wants from you, and quickly respond to it. Unlike the culture around you, always dragging you down to its level of immaturity, God brings the best out of you, develops well-formed maturity in you.*
>
> ~Rom. 12:1, 2 (MSG)

One sentence in particular catches my attention on a fairly regular basis:

"Don't become so well-adjusted to your culture that you fit into it without even thinking." It is counter-balanced with the sentence that states, *"Unlike the culture around you, always dragging you down to its level of immaturity..."*

To unpack those two narratives, consider this:

The first directive refers to the culture we're in. The wording of "your culture" isn't referring to the culture we're from—that is to say—the culture of our native homeland, God's kingdom, the "as it is in heaven" one. That's the culture we're called to represent, just as our Lord was *called to* when he arrived here.

Jesus said, *"I must preach the good news of the kingdom of God to*

the other towns as well; for I was sent for this purpose." (Lu. 4:43)

It also says that it is possible to fit into the temporal culture of the world "without even thinking." In other words, becoming so accustomed to the way(s) things are done here can take place by not giving it a thought. Fitting in here—socially, culturally, politically—can become the normal way of living, as opposed to representing the way(s) of Kingdom *otherness* that we are here to model. That's the "in the world, not of it" model that believers are called out to represent here on earth (Jn. 15:19, Jn. 17:15, 16). (See also 2 Cor. 5:18-21 / Eph. 5:8 / Col. 3:17 / 2 Peter 2:9.)

The second directive says that the surrounding culture of the world is "always dragging us down to its level of immaturity." That dynamic is in direct opposition to what the Scriptures say is to be one of the main goals for followers of Christ. Here are two examples that address that:

We are to:

> *"...attain to the unity of the faith and of the knowledge of the Son of God, to mature manhood, to the measure of the stature of the fullness of Christ, so that we may no longer be children, tossed to and fro by the waves and carried about by every wind of doctrine, by human cunning, by craftiness in deceitful schemes."*
>
> ~Eph. 4:13, 14

The next verse (15) says in part that we are to *"grow up into Christ...."*

What's being addressed here is the *process of maturing* as believers. And, our ability to mature in the faith is directly hampered by the downward pull of the worlds [world's] culture toward immaturity.

I pose that the key issue that serves to slow down (or block) that process is a lack of personal priority in our pursuit of the kingdom of God and his righteousness. Such a quest is to be based on the "seek first" that Jesus declared as the #1 objective for the ordering of our lives and lifestyles. In order to do that, our plans and

purposes must remain open to what I call *adaptive recalibrating*. Followers of Christ should remember to check their coordinates, and make course corrections as needed in order to reach their desired destination.

Here's a road marker to take note of:

Thus says the Lord: 'Stand by the roads, and look, and ask for the ancient paths, where the good way is; and walk in it...'

~Jer. 6:16

Addendum

There is one Biblical story in particular that has illuminated my spiritual pathway with a glow that emanates from the inside out. It offers a glimpse of the dynamics that can move us from where we are to where we're purposed to go. To do so, some serious recalibration had to take place in the process.

Here's the story, and the process it entails:

CLOSER TO THE CLOUD
(Ex. 13:17-22)

If your presence doesn't go before us
We're not moving, we're stayin' here
If your fire doesn't light our path
Then this is where we'll be
Until we know you've made a way
We'll keep resting, and waiting Lord
[resting and waiting, Lord]
Listening till we hear you say, "Child, it's time"

CHORUS:
Draw me closer to the cloud when it starts movin'
Closer to the heart of what you're doin'
Closer to the kingdom I'm pursuing
Draw me closer to the cloud

If the glory of your holy hand isn't on me
Then I'm undone
How else can I fulfill your plan
Without your precious touch
No one else will understand
It's your presence that changes me
So Father, this is where I'll stand until it's time
REPEAT CHORUS

~W. Berry / See & Say Songs, BMI

From Manifest Presence to Indwelling Presence

The story (the backstory) originates in Exodus 13:17-22. Another indicator of how the process is mentioned in Exodus 14:20. Then the narrative resumes again in Exodus 33:7-16.

Before I share my observations regarding the story in the text mentioned above, I first need to very briefly consider the principle (theological concept) of omnipresence.

The basic consensus defining *omnipresence* is:

1. The state of being widespread or constantly encountered.
2. The presence of God everywhere at the same time.

~Webster's Dictionary

I would say, everywhere, all the time. Or, stated as a question, *Where is God not?* The answer is that there is nowhere He isn't. I would support that perspective using Psalm 139:7-12 which declares:

> *"Where shall I go from your Spirit? Or where shall I flee from your presence? If I ascend to heaven, you are there! If I make my bed in Sheol, you are there! If I take the wings of the morning and dwell in the uttermost parts of the sea, even there your hand shall lead me, and your right hand shall hold me. If I say, "Surely the darkness shall cover me, and the light about me be night," even the darkness is not dark to you; the night is bright as the day, for darkness is as light with you."*

Now, on to the story of Jehovah, Moses, the pillar of fire, the cloud of presence, and recalibration:

> *"When Pharaoh let the people go, God did not lead them by way of the land of the Philistines, although that was near. For God said, "Lest the people change their minds when they see war and return to Egypt." But God led the people around by the way of the wilderness toward the Red Sea. And the people*

of Israel went up out of the land of Egypt equipped for battle. Moses took the bones of Joseph with him, for Joseph had made the sons of Israel solemnly swear, saying, "God will surely visit you, and you shall carry up my bones with you from here." And they moved on from Succoth and encamped at Etham, on the edge of the wilderness. And the Lord went before them by day in a pillar of cloud to lead them along the way, and by night in a pillar of fire to give them light, that they might travel by day and by night. The pillar of cloud by day and the pillar of fire by night did not depart from before the people."

~Ex. 13:17-22

As I read the Scriptures, I see no comprehension of the theological concept of omnipresence active at the time of the story presented here. In fact, I see no understanding of omnipresence at work in the lives of Adam and Eve or their descendants either. I believe that's because Jehovah chose to reveal Himself through external manifestations theophanies rather than an indwelling awareness. Those external manifestations served as a witness to God's *everywhereness*. And, that manner of being seems to have served as all that was needed for those who were to follow Him to do just that—follow Him by following the signs He provided.

The coordinates that Jehovah gave for Moses to follow were based on the manifestation of a pillar of fire (by day), and the cloud (at night). When they moved, so did the people. When they remained stationary, the people set up their tents and settled. That process was clearly and distinctly set forth for them to follow (Num. 9:17). How they were to move was based solely on God's presence moving and leading His people manifestly. Their task was based on obedience to the directive they could see and track. The narrative in the text makes that plain—at least to me.

Hence, the pillar of fire by day, [remove comma] and the cloud by night served to assure, protect, and guide Moses and the wilderness children through the desert and on to the "Promised Land."

145

That perspective leads me to the *adaptive recalibrating* that took place in Moses' life. He had to adjust to a new method of following Jehovah—from following the manifestations of the pillar of fire and the overcovering cloud—to an altogether *otherness*. Both of those symbols had served as tangible evidences that validated the *Presence* as being with the wilderness children on their sojourn toward (and into) the "Promised Land." There is a key passage that provides a clear perspective in regards to when (and how) that necessary realignment took place. I'll unpack it here.

For context, read Exodus 33:1-11. Following that, here's where the recalibration begins to take place:

> *Moses said to the Lord, "See, you say to me, 'Bring up this people,' but you have not let me know whom you will send with me. Yet you have said, 'I know you by name, and you have also found favor in my sight.' Now therefore, if I have found favor in your sight, please show me now your ways, that I may know you in order to find favor in your sight. Consider too that this nation is your people." And he said, "My presence will go with you, and I will give you rest." And he said to him, "If your presence will not go with me, do not bring us up from here. For how shall it be known that I have found favor in your sight, I and your people? Is it not in your going with us, so that we are distinct, I and your people, from every other people on the face of the earth?"*
>
> ~Exodus 33:12-16

NOTE: What follows is not an exhaustive theological exposition. Rather, it is based on my limited understanding, as best I can narrate it.

I find Moses' prayer in Exodus 33:12-16 to be one of the most important and astounding presented in the entire Bible. In essence, his request is for Jehovah's abiding presence to sustain him and God's people. He is not asking for any sort of physical

representation to manifest. The reason(s) for his request are twofold. They deserve some serious consideration, because what he asks for is not only answered in and among the wilderness children, it continues to be actively extended and imparted still today. Let me explain:

As to the reason(s) for his prayerful intercessory request, there are:

1. He was seeking Presence for himself. *"...for how shall it be known that I have favor in your sight...?* (v.16a)
2. He was seeking it on behalf of the people as well. *"...I and your people..."* (v.16a)

Those two interlinked requests tell us *what* Moses wanted—abiding presence for himself and for the people (the nation) of Israel. However, what he says just after those requests provides us with the *why*.

"Is it not in your going with us, so that we are distinct, I and your people, from every other people on the face of the earth?" (v.16b)

Here's where the astounding part comes in. The word *distinct* (ESV) is rendered as *separated* in the KJV. In Hebrew it means, *shown as different; marvelous, set apart; to make as being wonderful.*

Moses' prayer on behalf of himself, the nation of Israel, and (by extension) to all those who were to follow Jehovah thereafter, wasn't for provision, protection, healing, victory, blessing, deliverance, or such. Nope! It was for one singularly specific thing—*abiding/ indwelling presence!* And, the reason for such a desire wasn't based on any sort of self-serving, self-entitled need Moses (or the people) had.

It was so that they would be distinctively known by those they were to come into contact with in the days, months, decades, and centuries to come. In other words, the request for indwelling presence alone was to serve as a "witness" to anyone and everyone who had no knowledge of or relationship with the Father, Son, and Holy Ghost. I pose to you that the very thing Moses ask [asked] for is the very thing that should be the distinctive in the lives of those who consider themselves to be followers of the Lord, Christ Jesus, through the power of the Holy Ghost (Acts 1:8).

What I am saying is that the dynamics of Pentecost mentioned in Acts 1:8 transpired as a direct result of the Exodus 33 prayer that Moses prayed. That verse is outworked this way:

"You shall receive power, after that the Holy Ghost has come upon you: and you will [ye shall] be witnesses unto me both in Jerusalem, and in all Judaea, and in Samaria, and unto the uttermost part of the earth."

(KJV)

To me, the sequential process is best understood as unfolding like this:

Presence proceeds Power / Power prompts Witness / Witness proclaims Testimony / Testimony produces Revival.

Believers are to *be* witnesses. They are made (or transformed) into witness beings not witness doings. Witnesses declare what they know and believe directly through their witness. That's what witnesses do, they witness. A witness is a being, witnessing is what a witness does. That is exactly what Moses requested that God would do on behalf of (for the sake of) His own name.

God's answer to Moses' prayer is still at work in the very same way today as it was when that prayer was offered up.

"Know ye not that ye are the temple of God, and that the Spirit of God dwelleth in you?"

~1 Cor. 3:16 (KJV)
(See also Col. 3:17)

Perhaps the best New Testament narrative in support of what I've just narrated is found in 1 Peter 2:9 which says:

"But you are God's "chosen generation," his "royal priesthood," his "holy nation," his "peculiar people"—all the old titles of God's people now belong to you. It is for you now to demonstrate the

goodness of him who has called you out of darkness into his
amazing light. In the past you were not "a people" at all: now
you are the people of God. In the past you had no experience of
his mercy, but now it is intimately yours."

(Phillips)

So if you're serious about living this new resurrection life with
Christ, act like it. Pursue [keep seeking / Mt. [insert space]6:33]
the things over which Christ presides. Don't shuffle along, eyes
to the ground, absorbed with the things right in front of you.
Look up, and be alert to what is going on around Christ—that's
where the action is. See things from his perspective. Your old
life is dead. Your new life, which is your real life—even though
invisible to spectators—is with Christ in God. He is your life.
When Christ (your real life, remember) shows up again on
this earth, you'll show up, too—the real you, the glorious you.
Meanwhile, be content with obscurity, like Christ.

~Col. 3:1-4 (MSG) emphasis added

"It shall come to pass in the latter days that the mountain of
the house of the Lord shall be established as the highest of the
mountains, and it shall be lifted up above the hills; and peoples
shall flow to it, and many nations shall come, and say: "Come,
let us go up to the mountain of the Lord, to the house of the
God of Jacob, that he may teach us his ways and that we may
walk in his paths." For out of Zion shall go forth the law, and
the word of the Lord from Jerusalem. He shall judge between
many peoples, and shall decide disputes for strong nations far
away; and they shall beat their swords into plowshares, and
their spears into pruning hooks; nation shall not lift up sword
against nation, neither shall they learn war anymore; but they
shall sit every man under his vine and under his fig tree, and
no one shall make them afraid, for the mouth of the Lord of
hosts has spoken. ***For all the peoples walk each in the name of***

its god, but we will walk in the name of the Lord our God forever and ever."

~Micah 4:1-5 emphasis added

Go well, be well.

~Old African salutation

ADDENDUM II

(7/3/2022)

In the process of wrapping up this manuscript, I've been reading from the collective works of S. D. Gordon as a devotional. *His Quite Talks* (published in 1904 or thereabouts) have served as a sort of *Ebenezer, helping me to chart my journey. I came across the following insightful comments that seemed to fit just fine with what I've been addressing in the constriction of this book.

*A commemoration of divine assistance

"We are to remain in the world for its sake, but to allow nothing in it to disturb our full touch with the other world where our citizenship is, The Christian's position in this world is strikingly like that of a nation's ambassador at a foreign court...

...now we are strangers, sojourners, indeed more, ambassadors, representatives of a government foreign to the present prince of this world. It is only as we keep in perfect sympathy with the homeland and its Head that there can flow into and through us all the immeasurable power of our King...

...aggressive earnestness does not mean noise and dust, shuffling of feet, and bustling confusion. It means rather the

steady, steady movement of the sun which noiselessly, dust-lessly, moves onward, hour after hour, day in and day out, regardless of any storms, or disturbances. It means the quiet, peaceful, but resistless uninterrupted movement of the moon rising night after night, and going through its circle of action. Earnestness means the burning of the inner spirit. Its fires dim not, for they are fed continually from secret sources…

…some people are bounded by the horizon of the town where they live, some by the particular church to which they belong, some the denomination. Some the state, or even the nation. Jesus fixes the horizon of His followers as that of the world. Jesus was visionary. He talked about all nations, a race, a world."

~From *Quiet Talks On Service*
(Published in 1906)
S. D. Gordon

Wayne Berry

Pondering(s)
Pondering(s) Too
Particular Pondering(s)

Each of those books served as narrative construction sites upon which pathways (roadways) were built. Those pathway(s) provided road maps of a sort, as part of the *questing* I continue to navigate. They've helped to guide me from where I was to where I'm headed. They are available through several online outlets.

Seek and find.

also available from

WordCrafts Press

Deconstructing a Disciples Doubt
Dr. Jason Lee McKinney, EdD

What's the Big Idea?
Robert G. Lee

I Wish Someone Had Told Me
Barbie Loflin

Finding God in the Bathroom
Dr. Brian C. Johnson, PhD

www.wordcrafts.net